CONTENTS

ISBN: 0-673-14503-4

910-RRC-939291908988

ENGLISH
FOR A CHANGING WORLD

AUTHORS   Caroline Banks • Sandra Briggs

Jann Huizenga • Constance Peterson

Judy Veramendi

Consulting Reviewers

Professor Augusto Baratau
American Language School
Guayaquil, Ecuador

Professor Pilar Díaz Múgica
Centro de Estudios Universitarios San Pablo
Madrid, Spain

Dr. Mitsuo Hashimoto
Aoyama Gakuin University
Tokyo, Japan

Maricelle Meyer
G. Zirides Athena School
Athens, Greece

Sally Anderson Ochoa
Fundación Colegio Americano de Puebla
Puebla, Mexico

Diane E. Özbal
Robert College
Istanbul, Turkey

Professor Guillermo Sáenz
Instituto de Lenguas Extranjeras S.A.
San Jose, Costa Rica

Maurice Sullivan
ESL/Bilingual Consultant
Chicago, Illinois

SCOTT, FORESMAN AND COMPANY
Editorial Office Glenview, Illinois

Regional Offices Palo Alto, California   Tucker, Georgia
Glenview, Illinois   Oakland, New Jersey   Dallas, Texas

USING THE CUE BOOK

1. Open the Cue Book to the Chart
mentioned in the exercise
directions in the Student Book.

XX: Ask and answer.
Use Cue Book Chart 4.

2. Read the cue for the model in the
Student Book and find the correct
picture in the Cue Book Chart.
Then read the model.

cue: **1**/at work

model: STUDENT A Where's the <u>accountant</u>?
           STUDENT B <u>She's</u> <u>at work</u>.

3. Look at item number 1 in the
exercise and repeat the above
procedure, finding the correct
picture and making the correct
substitutions in the model.
Continue with the other
numbered items. (Note: the
sequence will not always start
with Picture 1.)

1. **2**/at home
STUDENT A Where's the <u>painter</u>?
STUDENT B <u>He's</u> <u>at home</u>.
2. **3**/at school
STUDENT C Where's the <u>architect</u>?
STUDENT D <u>He's</u> <u>at school</u>.

LESSON 1

I think I'm lost!

CONVERSATIONS

1.

MOLLY   Excuse me. I want to register for English. Is this the right line?

BILLY   Yes, it is. Just stand behind me.

MOLLY   Thanks. I'm new here, and I thought I was lost.

BILLY   I'm new, too. Let's register together.

MOLLY   Good idea. My name's Molly Burton.

BILLY   Hi. I'm Billy Taylor.

2.

MOLLY   I want to register for English III.

TEACHER   Fine. Just fill out this form.

MOLLY   What time is the class?

TEACHER   1:30, in Room 210. The teacher is Mr. Shakespeare.

MOLLY   Thank you.

3.

TEACHER   Can I help you?

BILLY   Oh, I think we're in the wrong class!

TEACHER   This is Math IV. What class are you looking for?

BILLY   English III. It's at 2:10 in Room 130. Isn't this Room 130?

Questions

1. Were Molly and Billy old friends?
2. Was English III at 2:10 in Room 130?
3. How do you register at your school?

VOCABULARY

New Words   See page 142 for abbreviations.

1. **earth**   2. **form**   3. **handwriting**

to col lect', *v.* to bring together; to put together: *We collected wood for a fire.*

to cor rect', *v.* to show the mistakes in something: *The teacher corrected the papers.*

course(s), *n.* a group of classes about one thing: *Ms. Melba is teaching two music courses this year.*

to de fine', *v.* to explain: *The dictionary defines words.*

to de scribe', *v.* to tell or write about: *The reporter described the fire.*

to dis cuss', *v.* to talk about: *They discussed their plans for the picnic.*

earth, *n. We live on the earth.* See Picture 1.

to fail, *v.* to not pass; to get a very low grade on a test or course: *He failed the test because he didn't study.*

form(s), *n.* a piece of paper with places to write on: *I filled out the application form.* See Picture 2.

ge og'ra phy, *n.* the studying of the earth: *We learned about Spain in our geography class.*

glad, *adj.* happy: *He's glad because he won the game.*

to hand' in', *v.* to give or deliver something to somebody: *The students handed in their homework before class.*

hand'writ'ing, *n. Everybody can read Susan's handwriting.* See Picture 3.

just, *adv.* 1. only: *Just give the cashier your money, and she'll give you a ticket.* 2. not very long ago: *He just came home.*

to mean, *v.* to want to say: Huge *means "very big."*

to pass, *v.* to not fail; to get a good grade on a test or course: *She passed the test because she studied.*

to pro nounce', *v.* to say: *The teacher pronounced the words for the class.*

to reg'is ter, *v.* to write a name in a list: *Mr. and Mrs. Smith registered at the hotel.*

reg'is tra'tion, *n.* registering: *Registration for classes will be next Thursday.*

sci'ence(s), *n.* a careful studying of something: *Geography and math are sciences.*

so, *adv.* See Grammar.

sor'ry, *adj.* sad: *I'm sorry because I lost my books.*

test(s), *n.* a list of questions: *We have a math test on Friday.*

to write' down', *v.* to write: *Write down the questions in your notebooks.*

Idioms

Excuse me. Can you help me?

Excuse me.

Excuse me. I'm *very* sorry.

Excuse me. I have to answer the phone.

take + noun

Do you **take the bus** to work? No, I **take the train.**

I **took history** last year. This year I want to **take a course** in geography.

We're **taking tests** in science and math tomorrow.

She **took the part of** the grandmother in the school play.

He **takes a bath (a shower)** every morning.

We're going to **take a trip** to Greece.

Word Study

new/old

I've known him for a long time. We're **old** friends.

We just moved to this town. We're **new** here. Our children have a lot of **new** friends.

Thanks/Thank you

Say **Thanks** to your friends and family. (This is INFORMAL.)

Say **Thank you** to your teachers and other adults. (This is FORMAL.)

two-word verbs

hand in We **handed in** our papers. OR We **handed** our papers **in.**

We **handed** them **in.**

write down Please **write down** your name. OR Please **write** your name **down.**

Please **write** it **down.**

Principal Parts of Verbs

base form	present participle	past tense	past participle
col lect	col lect ing	col lect ed	col lect ed
cor rect	cor rect ing	cor rect ed	cor rect ed
de fine	de fin ing	de fined	de fined
de scribe	de scrib ing	de scribed	de scribed
dis cuss	dis cuss ing	dis cussed	dis cussed
fail	fail ing	failed	failed
hand in	hand ing in	hand ed in	hand ed in
mean	mean ing	meant	meant
pass	pass ing	passed	passed
pro nounce	pro nounc ing	pro nounced	pro nounced
reg is ter	reg is ter ing	reg is tered	reg is tered
write down	writ ing down	wrote down	writ ten down

Pronunciation   Sentence rhythm; sentences with Key Words PLEASE /i/, SIT /ɪ/, NAME /e/, PEN /ɛ/, CLASS /æ/, FINE /ɑɪ/

I'm **afraid** I'm going to **fail,**
But I'd **really** like to **pass.**
I can **register** for **Spanish;**
I can **take** another **class.**
I'll **make** an **application.**
I don't **have** to study **math!**

The **English** teacher **says, "Define!"**
And **we explain** each **line.**
The **science** teacher **says, "Describe!"**
It's **yellow, big,** and **high.**
The **history** teacher **says, "Explain!"**
And **means,** "Tell **when,** and **why.**"

Vocabulary Exercise

Choose the correct word.

collected	1. Ms. Melba is happy because everybody _____ her course.
corrects	2. For your homework, _____ your room at home.
define	3. Molly's unhappy because she _____ the geography test.
describe	4. The TV reporter couldn't _____ the names of the cities.
discussing	5. The teacher uses a red pencil when she _____ papers.
failed	6. Billy's _____ for Spanish III.
mean	7. What does this word mean? Please _____ it for me.
passed	8. He _____ the ticket money from all of the students.
pronounce	9. The students were _____ the science test.
registering	10. What did he _____ when he said that?

GRAMMAR

Clauses after *I think, I'm glad, I'm sorry*

Look at the verb tenses carefully.
A present tense, a past tense, or a future tense can follow a present tense.

I think *(now)* it**'s raining** *(now)*.
I'm glad *(now)* you**'re** here. *(now)*.
I'm sorry *(now)* your team **isn't winning** *(now)*.

I think *(now)* I **left** my glasses on the table *(before now)*.
I'm glad *(now)* they **were waiting** for me *(before now)*.
He's sorry *(now)* he **didn't go** to Molly's party *(before now)*.

I think *(now)* we**'re going to have** a test today *(later)*.
We're glad *(now)* you**'re going to go** with us *(later)*.
She's sorry *(now)* she **won't be** at the party *(later)*.

Do you think *(now)* you**'ll visit** Europe *(next year)?*
Yes, I think so *(now)*. OR Yes, I **think** *(now)* we **will** *(later)*.
No, I don't think so *(now)*. OR No, I **don't think** *(now)* we **will** *(later)*.

A past tense follows a past tense.

I **thought** *(before now)* I **was** lost *(at the same time)*.
She **thought** *(before now)* she **had** her books with her *(at the same time)*.
He **didn't think** *(before now)* the students **were studying** *(at the same time)*.

She **was glad** *(before now)* she **knew** Spanish *(at the same time)*.
We **were sorry** *(before now)* you **were sick** *(at the same time)*.
I **was glad** *(before now)* it **wasn't snowing** *(at the same time)*.

That can come after *think, glad,* or *sorry.*

I think **that** it's raining.
We're glad **that** you came.
She was sorry **that** she was late.

Exercises

1A: **Subject pronouns.** Ask and answer. Use Cue Book Chart 1.

2/English/geography
   STUDENT A Do you think you'll take English next year?
   STUDENT B No, I think I'll take geography.

1. **3**/art/math
2. **4**/science/music
3. **6**/history/art
4. **7**/geography/Spanish
5. **2**/French/science

1B: *Glad/sorry.* Choose the correct words.

I'm glad   **I'm sorry**

1. _____ I found the right room.
2. _____ you can't read my handwriting.
3. _____ I got a good grade on the geography test.
4. _____ she broke her leg.
5. _____ he could help you.

1C: *Glad/sorry.* Make a new sentence. Use *I'm glad* or *I'm sorry*. Use *because*.

You went to the party. You had a wonderful time.
I'm glad I went to the party because I had a wonderful time.

1. You didn't study. You failed the math test.
2. You went to that movie. It wasn't very good.
3. The geography test was easy. You got a good grade.
4. It's time for lunch. You're hungry.
5. You're taking this course. It's very difficult.

1D: **Object pronouns/time.** Ask and answer. Tell when. Use Cue Book Chart 1.

> **1**/6:15 STUDENT A When will you meet <u>me</u>?
> STUDENT B At <u>six-fifteen</u>.

1. **3**/7.30	3. **5**/3:20	5. **1**/4:00	7. **4**/8:30	9. **7**/2:40
2. **4**/10:00	4. **7**/5:45	6. **3**/noon	8. **5**/9:15	10. **1**/11:10

1E: **Past tense.** Make a sentence. Use Cue Book Chart 2.

sorry/**1**/all those sour apples
<u>I'm sorry I ate all those sour apples.</u>

1. glad/**2**/that glass of milk	6. sorry/**7**/the wrong lesson
2. glad/**3**/my new car	7. glad/**8**/my bike to the picnic
3. sorry/**4**/my old house	8. sorry/**9**/that angry letter
4. glad/**5**/that bookcase	9. glad/**10**/carefully
5. sorry/**6**/that ugly picture	10. sorry/**1**/five sandwiches

COMMUNICATION PRACTICE

Guided Conversation

STUDENT A What course are you registering for?
STUDENT B <u>Geography</u>.
STUDENT A What time is the class?
STUDENT B At <u>ten o'clock</u> in Room <u>3</u>.
STUDENT A Who's teaching it?
STUDENT B <u>Mr. Magellan.</u> He's a very good teacher.
STUDENT A I don't have a class at <u>ten o'clock</u>.
I think I'll take <u>geography</u>, too.

LIST OF COURSES			
Class	*Time*	*Room*	*Teacher*
science	8:00	15	Mrs. Curie
English	9:00	4	Mr. Shakespeare
math	9:00	7	Ms. Einstein
geography	10:00	3	Mr. Magellan
history	10:00	12	Miss Tudor
art	11:00	9	Mr. Picasso
music	11:00	2	Ms. Melba

Activities

A. Ask somebody.

What's your favorite class?
What time is it?
Who's the teacher?
Why do you like that class?

B. Talk with somebody.

1. You want to register for Math III, and you think you're lost. You're looking for the right line, and a student helps you. Perform this conversation with another student. (You can use sentences from Conversation 1.)

2. A student is registering for school and a teacher is helping. The students chooses a course and asks a lot of questions. You and a friend take the part of the student and the teacher and perform their conversation. The student will ask, "Is the class large or small? Is the work hard or easy? Is there a lot of homework? Are there a lot of tests?"

C. What do you think?

Are you glad or sorry you're studying English?
Why are you glad or sorry?

Maybe you can use . . .

easy	go on a trip
hard	get a job
interesting	talk with friends
important	study very hard

Self Test

Choose the correct word.

courses
earth
failed
form
geography
grades
handwriting
registration
science
tests

1. We learned about the _____ in our geography class.
2. We filled out the _____ forms.
3. He didn't study, so he _____ five courses.
4. Molly always gets good _____ on her tests.
5. Who's teaching the art _____?
6. I'm glad he typed his paper, because I can't read his _____.
7. The teacher corrected our _____.
8. Please fill out this _____ and hand it in.
9. We learned about Russia in our _____ class.
10. I'm taking a _____ course about animals.

LESSON 2

Would you like to go with me?

CONVERSATIONS

1.

MOLLY What are you going to do after school?

BILLY I'm going to go to the soccer game. Would you like to go with me?

MOLLY Thanks. I'd love to, but I can't. I have to go shopping.

BILLY We can do that on the way to the stadium.

MOLLY Good idea. I'll see you after school.

2.

MOLLY Excuse me, sir. Can you help me?

CLERK Certainly. What can I do for you?

MOLLY I need a new cassette player.

CLERK Fine. What do you need it for?

MOLLY To listen to the tapes for my English class. My old one doesn't sound good. I can't understand the words.

CLERK Perhaps you'd like this one. It's not very expensive, and your cassettes will sound great. Would you like to try it?

MOLLY Yes, I would. Here's one of my cassettes.

3.

BILLY Boy, that was a terrific game! But now I have to go home and do my English assignment.

MOLLY Me, too. Would you like to listen to the tapes on my new cassette player?

BILLY Sure. Then we can help each other.

Questions

1. Why couldn't Molly go to the game?
2. What did she need a new cassette player for?
3. How do you and your friends help each other?

VOCABULARY

New Words

2. **computer**

1. **calculator**

3. **stadium**

ab′sent, *adj.* not here: *Three members of the class are absent today.*

to ac cept′, *v.* to say yes to: *She asked me to her party, and I accepted her invitation.*

to bor′row, *v.* to take and use for a short time: *I borrowed a book from the library.*

boy, *interj.* wow: *Boy, that cake tastes good!*

cal′cu la′tor(s), *n. Please add these numbers on your calculator.* See Picture 1.

cer′tain ly, *adv.* yes; sure: *Will you help me? Certainly.*

com put′er(s), *n. A computer figured out the students' class schedules.* See Picture 2.

to find′ out′, *v.* to learn about; to learn for the first time: *We found out a lot about the ocean in our science class.*

fine, *adj.* very good: *She's a fine student.*
adv. very well: *I'm doing fine.*

to go out′ with, *v.* to go (to a party or a show) with: *My sister doesn't go out with boys because she's too young.*

grad′u a′tion(s), *n.* graduating: *When I finished high school, my parents came to my graduation.*

to im prove′, *v.* to make (something) better: *The editor improved the directions for the exercise.*

op′po site(s), *n.* See Word Study.

per haps′, *adv.* maybe: *Perhaps I can help you.*

pres′ent, *adj.* here: *All of the students are present today.*

prin′ci pal(s), *n.* the most important person in a school: *The principal planned a meeting for all of the teachers.*

same, *adj.* See Word Study.

sched′ule(s), *n.* a list with times and dates: *The schedule of our team's soccer games is on the bulletin board.*

sta′di um(s), *n. Our team plays its games in the stadium.* See Picture 3.

sup plies′, *n.* things to use: *Our school gets its supplies of books, paper, pencils, and chalk from the city.*

ter rif′ic, *adj.* wonderful: *Your party was terrific!*

way(s), *n.* how to go; street; avenue: *Do you know the way to the post office?*

what′ for′, *adv.* why: *What did you do that for?*

Idioms

They're watching **each other.**

They're going to the stadium.
They're **on the way** to the stadium.

Word Study

the opposite/the same

Use **of** after **the opposite.** *New* is **the opposite of** *old.*
Use **as** after **the same.** *Present* is **the same as** *here.*

maybe/perhaps

INFORMAL   **Maybe** Molly and I will go to the movies.
FORMAL   **Perhaps** you'd like coffee with your dessert, sir.

ways to say *yes*

CUSTOMER   Can you help me,
ma'am?

WAITRESS   **Certainly.** (FORMAL)

CLERK   We'll deliver the flowers
tomorrow.

CUSTOMER   **Fine.** (FORMAL)

YOUR BROTHER   Will you help me, Billy?
YOU   **Sure.** (INFORMAL)

HUSBAND   Let's have steak for dinner.
WIFE   **OK.** (INFORMAL)

what for

MOLLY   I'm going to the store.
BILLY   **What for?**
MOLLY   I need a new cassette.
BILLY   **What** do you need it **for?**

Principal Parts of Verbs

base form	present participle	past tense	past participle
ac cept	ac cept ing	ac cept ed	ac cept ed
bor row	bor row ing	bor rowed	bor rowed
find out	find ing out	found out	found out
go out with	go ing out with	went out with	gone out with
im prove	im prov ing	im proved	im proved

/-	MAYbe we can BORrow the SCHEDule.	I'm **sorry** that the **coffee** isn't **hot.**
-/	PerHAPS you'll acCEPT these supPLIES.	I put **water** and some **coffee** in the **pot.**
/--	The PRINcipal's at the STAdium.	Turn it **on? Oh!** I **forgot!**
-/-	They're imPROVing this terRIFic comPUTer.	Did Ann **choose** these **sugar cookies?**
/---	There's a CALculátor on the DICtionáry.	I don't **know,** but I'll find **out.**
--/-	Here's an ínviTAtion to my gráduAtion.	Let's **just discuss** the **soup.**

Vocabulary Exercise

Choose the correct word.

✗ **absent**	1.	The office _____ are in the cabinet.
✗ **calculator**	2.	The _____ ordered new books for the school.
computers	3.	We'll watch the game at the _stadium_
found out	4.	I can't do my math because my _calculator_ is broken.
✗ **graduation**	5.	There's a mistake on my class _____.
principal	✗ 6.	Tom was _____ because he was sick.
schedule	7.	After the _____, the students went to a party.
✗ **stadium**	8.	She _graduated_ her grade for her English class.
supplies	9.	They ate their sandwiches on the _____ to school.
way	10.	Some _____ can correct tests.

GRAMMAR

1. Infinitives of purpose

An infinitive is *to* + the base form of a verb: *to know, to pronounce, to register.* Look at these sentences with infinitives:

I need a cassette player **to play** my tapes.
He went downtown **to buy** some supplies.
They made a fire **to cook** their food.

These infinitives are infinitives of purpose.
Infinitives of purpose answer the question *"why?"*

People often use this short form in conversations:

Why did they go to the stadium?
To watch the soccer game.

2. Short form of infinitives

People use this short form in conversations, too:

"Didn't you do your homework?" "No, I forgot **to** (do it)."
"Have you seen that new movie?" "No, and I'm not going **to** (see it)."

Exercises

2A: **Possessive adjective pronouns.** Ask and answer. Use Cue Book Chart 1.

> **2**/Monday/read/book
> STUDENT A What would you like to do on Monday?
> STUDENT B I'd like to read my book.

1. **3**/Tuesday/listen to/tapes
2. **4**/Wednesday/paint/house
3. **6**/Thursday/register for/classes
4. **7**/Friday/go out with/friends
5. **2**/Saturday/plan/graduation party

2B: **Infinitives of purpose.** Choose the correct ending for each sentence.

1. He listened to the tapes	a. to watch the soccer game.
2. She went to the office	b. to find out our grades.
3. They went to the stadium	c. to meet the principal.
4. I need some chalk	d. to improve his English.
5. We can use the computer	e. to write on the blackboard.

2C: **Infinitives of purpose.** Ask and answer. Use Cue Book Chart 2. Start with **3.**

> go to the store/**3**/a ruler
> STUDENT A Why did you go to the store?
> STUDENT B To buy a ruler.

1. make those hats/**4**/at the market
2. need that wood/**5**/a bookcase
3. bring that chalk/**6**/on the blackboard
4. go to the library/**7**/about computers
5. borrow his bike/**8**/to school yesterday
6. use my pen/**9**/a letter
7. buy a new car/**10**/to work
8. go to the cafeteria/**1**/lunch
9. make that lemonade/**2**/at the picnic
10. collect the money/**3**/the tickets

2D: Emphatic possessive pronouns. Ask and answer. Use Cue Book Chart 1.

ruler/**1**
    STUDENT A Whose <u>ruler</u> <u>is this</u>?
    STUDENT B <u>It's</u> <u>mine</u>.
erasers/**2**
    STUDENT C Whose <u>erasers</u> <u>are these</u>?
    STUDENT D <u>They're</u> <u>yours</u>.

1. cassettes/**3**
2. geography book/**4**
3. chalk/**5**
4. forms/**6**
5. handwriting/**7**
6. supplies/**1**
7. calculator/**2**
8. science test/**3**
9. schedule/**4**
10. grades/**5**

2E: Infinitives of purpose. Ask and answer.

The students went to the store because they wanted to buy some supplies.
    STUDENT A Where did <u>the students</u> go?
    STUDENT B <u>They went to the store to buy some supplies.</u>

1. The principal went to the post office because she wanted to send a package.
2. Billy went to the office because he wanted to use the computer.
3. They went to the stadium because they wanted to see the game.
4. Molly went to language school because she wanted to improve her English.
5. I went to the library because I wanted to borrow a book.

2F: Short form of infinitives. Ask and answer.

buy a ruler/need
    STUDENT A Are you going to <u>buy a ruler</u>?
    STUDENT B No, I don't <u>need</u> to.

1. see that movie/want
2. play tennis/want
3. go to the party/want
4. go home now/have
5. study for the test/need

2G: ***The same/the opposite.*** Make a sentence. Use *the same as* or *the opposite of.*

little/small   <u>*Little* is the same as *small.*</u>
old/new   <u>*Old* is the opposite of *new.*</u>

1. absent/present
2. pass/fail
3. big/large
4. right/wrong
5. old/young

6. smart/intelligent
7. hard/difficult
8. easy/difficult
9. rich/poor
10. scared/frightened

2H: ***Linking verbs.*** Make a sentence. Choose a word or phrase from each list.

a.	**b.**	**c.**
1. The flowers	tasted	terrific
2. The hot bread	smelled	terrible
3. The music	sounded	delicious
4. The pictures	looked	cold
5. The ground	felt	beautiful
6. The cassette		expensive
7. The coffee		great
8. The rain		wet
9. The towels		ugly
10. The cheese		wonderful

COMMUNICATION PRACTICE

Guided Conversation

STUDENT A What are you going to do on Saturday?
STUDENT B I'm going to go to City Park.
STUDENT A Oh? What for?
STUDENT B <u>To play tennis.</u> Would you like to go with me?
STUDENT A Terrific! I like to <u>play tennis.</u>

Activities

A. Ask somebody.

Where are you going after school?
Why are you going there?
Who's going to go with you?

B. Talk with somebody.

1. You're going to the movies tomorrow. Invite a friend. (You can use sentences from Conversation 1.)

2. A clerk in a department store is trying to sell a suitcase to a customer. You and a classmate take the parts of the clerk and the customer. The clerk will ask, "Do you want a big suitcase or a little one? What color do you want? What do you need a suitcase for?"

C. What do you think?

Where do you like to go with your friends?
What do you like to do?

Self Test

Choose a sentence to answer each question.

1. Why are you taking a conversation class?
2. What do you need a new suitcase for?
3. Why are you going to the music store?
4. Why did Fred buy a new suit?
5. What did the team go to the stadium for?
6. Why did you go to the principal's office?
7. What does she need a ruler for?
8. Why are you studying geography?
9. Why did the teacher collect the tests?
10. What did he borrow the calculator for?

a. To buy some new cassettes.
b. To practice soccer.
c. To get my schedule.
d. To improve my English.
e. To learn about the earth.
f. To take on my vacation.
g. To correct them.
h. To wear to his graduation.
i. To add all these numbers.
j. To measure the windows.

LESSON 3

What Does Your Handwriting Say About You?

READING

Is your handwriting large or small? Are your letters tall or short? Are your words and letters close to each other or are there big spaces* between them? Many people think the answers to these questions tell interesting things about you.

*space(s) an empty place

What does your handwriting mean? You can use graphology* to find out. Write a paragraph* in English on a piece of paper without lines*.

*graphology the studying of handwriting
*paragraph(s) See New Words.
*line(s) See Picture 1.

Now use a ruler to draw one line under the small letters, and another line on top of them. (See Picture 1.)

Are there big loops* in your top zone*? This means you have a lot of dreams and ideas. Would you like to be a writer or an artist? Large loops in the bottom zone mean you like to perform for an audience. Perhaps you'd like to be an actor or a dancer. Does your handwriting stay in the middle zone? You are a careful person and you work well with other people.

*loop(s) See Picture 1.
*zone(s) See Picture 1.

Which way do your letters slant*? Do they slant to the right? This means you like other people and you like to try new things. Perhaps your letters slant to the left. This means you are quiet and you don't want to be the same as other people. Some people's letters don't slant; they go up and down*. These people are good workers and don't get angry easily.

*to slant See Picture 2.

*up and down See Picture 2.

Look at the spaces between your letters and words. Big spaces mean you plan carefully. You like to read and to listen to music. Small spaces mean you like to talk. You enjoy other people and you like to be with them.

What does your handwriting say about you? Do you agree?

Questions

1. Why do people study graphology? How can you learn more about it?
2. What are the three zones in your handwriting? How can you find them?
3. Which way do your letters slant? What does that say about you? Do you agree?

VOCABULARY

New Words

1. *graphology*

— loop   top zone

middle zone

line   bottom zone

2. *quiet* — **slants to the left**   *grades* — **up and down**   *friendly* — **slants to the right**

ac′cent(s), *n.* the pronouncing of one syllable of a word louder than the others: *In letter the accent is on the first syllable.*

ac′cent mark′(s), *n.* a line (′) to show the loud syllable: *Put the accent mark on the second syllable.*

hy′phen(s), *n.* a short line (-) between two parts of a word: *There's a hyphen in the word* teen-ager.

line(s), *n.* 1. a number of words across a page: *There are 40 lines of handwriting on this page.* 2. *Draw a long line on your paper.* See Picture 1.

loud, *adv.* in a loud way: *Don't talk so loud.*

par′a graph(s), *n.* several sentences about the same idea: *There were six sentences in the paragraph about giraffes.*

syl′la ble(s), *n.* a word or a part of a word: *The word* register *has three syllables* (reg is ter).

Word Study

clauses after *know, mean, understand*

I think **it's going to rain.**

I know **it's going to rain.**

A lot of clouds usually means **it's going to rain.**

The baby doesn't understand **that it's going to rain.**

READING AND WRITING SKILLS

1. Alphabet
Capital letters: A, B, C, D, E, F, G, H, I, J, K, L, M, N, O, P, Q, R, S, T, U V, W, X, Y, Z
Small letters: a, b, c, d, e, f, g, h, i, j, k, l, m, n, o, p, q, r, s, t, u, v, w, x, y, z

2. Syllables
Every word has one or more syllables. *Test* has one syllable. *Discuss* has two syllables. *Registration* has four syllables. In the New Words list, there is a space between the syllables of a word: *dis cuss, reg is tra tion.*

When you are writing, you can break a word between syllables at the end of a line. Use a hyphen:

> I'm going to regis-
> ter for a course in sci-
> ence next year.

When you write:
1. Don't break a word with one syllable.
2. Break words with a hyphen only at the hyphen.
3. Don't leave only one letter on a line.

3. Accent
When a word has two or more syllables, you have to pronounce one syllable louder than the others. In the New Words list, the loudest syllable has an accent mark: *dis cuss′.* Some long words have a secondary (lighter) accent mark. Pronounce this syllable louder than the syllables without an accent mark, but not as loud as the syllable with the primary (darker) accent mark: *reg′is tra′tion.*

Exercises

3A: **Syllables.** Choose the word with the correct number of syllables.

basketball chess tennis
I like to play (3) .
I like to play basketball.

1. **cassette chalk eraser**
   Please give me that (1) .
2. **collected described failed**
   They (2) the tests.
3. **form handwriting schedule**
   I can't read this (3) .

art geography science
Are you going to take (2) ?
Are you going to take science?

4. **absent loud terrific**
   My students are (2) .
5. **corrected pronounced wrote**
   She (3) the vocabulary words.

3B: Syllables. Say these words. How many syllables does each one have?

1. school
2. assignment
3. behind
4. great
5. exciting
6. understand
7. absent
8. teacher
9. together
10. thought

3C: Accent. Say these words. Is the accent on the first, second, or third syllable?

1. par a graph
2. let ter
3. hy phen
4. syl la ble
5. dis cuss
6. ter rif ic
7. op po site
8. sci ence
9. com put er
10. sup plies

COMMUNICATION PRACTICE

Writing Activities

A. What does graphology say about you? Do you agree? Write three or four sentences about this. Look at the Reading for words and ideas.

B. Use graphology to learn about another person. Look at a paragraph of somebody's handwriting. Write several sentences about that person. You can use sentences from the Reading.

Unit Self Test

Make a new sentence.

She's in the principal's office. (I don't think so.)
I don't think she's in the principal's office.

1. He didn't fail the test. (I'm glad.)
2. They don't plan carefully. (I'm sorry.)
3. Geography is interesting. (I think so.)
4. I finished my homework. (I'm glad.)
5. The teacher's going to collect the papers. (I don't think so.)

Choose the correct ending for each sentence.

6. I need a pen
7. I called my friends
8. I went to the stadium
9. I borrowed a calculator
10. I need a cassette player

a. to invite them to my graduation.
b. to do my math.
c. to fill out the registration forms.
d. to play my tapes.
e. to watch the game.

LESSON 4

It's fun to drive.

CONVERSATIONS

1.

MR. TURNER My car is hard to steer, and the engine's making a terrible noise. Am I running out of gas?

ATTENDANT No. I think you need some oil.

MR. TURNER But I had some on my salad at lunch!

ATTENDANT Sir, the automobile needs oil, not you!

2.

ATTENDANT Excuse me. You need some air, too.

MR. TURNER No, I don't. It's cold out!

ATTENDANT You don't understand. Your front tire needs air. It's almost flat.

MR. TURNER Can you repair it?

ATTENDANT Oh, sure. It's easy to fix.

MR. TURNER Good. I'll open the hood again.

ATTENDANT Open the hood!?!? Did you just get your license?

MR. TURNER Why, yes. I got it yesterday. How did you know?

ATTENDANT Oh, I just guessed.

3.

ATTENDANT There you are, sir. Your car's fine now.

MR. TURNER Thank you. You've been very helpful.

ATTENDANT It was interesting to wait on you, sir!

Questions

1. Why was Mr. Turner's engine noisy?
2. Why did Mr. Turner need air?
3. Do you want to get a driver's license? What will you do when you get it?

VOCABULARY

New Words

1. The **air** is coming out of the **tire.**

2. She's putting **gas** in the car.

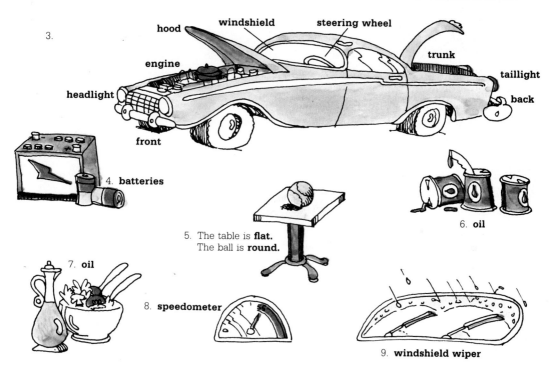

3.

4. **batteries**

5. The table is **flat.**
   The ball is **round.**

6. **oil**

7. **oil**

8. **speedometer**

9. **windshield wiper**

air, n. Birds and planes fly in the air. See Picture 1.

at ten'dant(s), n. The attendant is waiting on the customer. See Picture 2.

au'to mo bile'(s), n. a car: Mary drove her new automobile to work.

back(s), n. There's a bookcase at the back of the room. See Picture 3.

bat'ter y (batteries), n. His radio doesn't work because it needs a new battery. See Picture 4.

en'gine(s), n. Her car won't move because it needs a new engine. See Picture 3.

flat, adj. We can't play soccer here because the field isn't flat. See Picture 5.

front(s), n. He put a basket on the front of his bike. See Picture 3.

gas, n. They bought some gas for their truck. See Picture 2.

gas′ sta′tion(s), n. a place to buy gas: *The attendant at the gas station repaired my engine.*

to guess, v. to think "maybe" when you don't know: *I didn't know the correct answer, so I guessed.*

head′light′(s), n. *Always turn on your headlights when it's dark.* See Picture 3.

hood(s), n. *The engine is under the hood.* See Picture 3.

li′cense(s), n. a paper; you need a license to drive, fish, sell something, or do other things: *Mr. Brown can't drive his car because he doesn't have a driver's license.*

noise(s), n. something heard: *An alarm clock makes a loud noise.*

oil, n. 1. *Her car is old and uses a lot of oil.* See Picture 6. 2. *Did he cook the fish in oil or butter?* See Picture 7.

ped′al(s), n. *The gas pedal is on the floor of the car.* See Picture 1.

round, adj. *The wheel won't turn because it isn't round.* See Picture 5.

to run′ out′ of, v. to use all of; to have no more of: *We had to walk because we ran out of gas.*

speed om′e ter(s), n. *He called the mechanic because his speedometer was broken.* See Picture 8.

to steer, v. to turn (a car or bike) to the right or to the left: *She steered the car around a hole in the road.*

steer′ing wheel′(s), n. *Turn the steering wheel to the right.* See Picture 3.

tail′light′(s), n. *The taillights on most cars are red.* See Picture 3.

tire(s), n. *He took the tire off the wheel to fix it.* See Picture 3.

trunk(s), n. *Let's put the suitcases in the trunk.* See Picture 3.

why, interj. oh; yes; I see: *Why, it's cold out!*

wind′shield′(s), n. *She couldn't see because the windshield was very dirty.* See Picture 3.

wind′shield′ wip′er(s), n. *He turned on the windshield wipers when it started to rain.* See Picture 9.

Idioms

It's cold **out.** = It's cold outside.

The battery is **dead.** = The battery doesn't work.

Word Study

air

Mr. Robinson is sick.
He needs some **air.**

Mr. Robinson's front tire is flat.
It needs some **air.**

Principal Parts of Verbs

base form	present participle	past tense	past participle
guess	guess ing	guessed	guessed
run out of	run ning out of	ran out of	run out of
steer	steer ing	steered	steered

Pronunciation   Sentences with Key Words HERE /ɪr/, CHAIR /ɛr/, CHART /ɑr/, WORD /ɝ/, YOU'RE /ʊr/, DOOR /ɔr/; compound nouns

The **engineer steered near** the **cashier.**
They're going to **repair** the **stairs.**
The **architects** are at a **large party.**
The **nurse heard** the **first girl.**
You're figuring out **your** schedule.
Mr. **Gore** rode his **horse north.**

They'll fix the HEADlight at the GAS station.
Who put the BLUEbird in the BIRD cage?
The TAXI driver needs a new GAS pedal.
Did the MATH teacher give the SCIENCE test?
We'll have a BIRTHday party next WEEKend.
Show me the HANDwriting in that NOTEbook.

Vocabulary Exercise

Choose the correct word.

air	1. Bernice can't start her car because the _____ is dead.
battery	2. Alex put some _____ in his tire.
gas station	3. Mrs. Meyer turned on her _____ when it got dark.
guessed	4. She had to take a test to get her driver's _____.
headlights	5. You have to go to another bank. We've _____ money.
license	6. Margaret can't _____ the car because her arms are broken.
round	7. Beth put the packages in the _____ of her car and drove home.
run out of	8. He didn't know the answers to the exercise, so he _____.
steer	9. We don't have much gas. Let's find a _____.
trunk	10. The steering wheel in most automobiles is _____.

GRAMMAR

1. Adjective + infinitive

An adjective + infinitive comes after a form of *to be* and tells about the subject of the sentence.

I can drive this car easily. This car is **easy to drive.**
He could push the pedal easily. The pedal wasn't **hard to push.**
Computers are interesting. That new computer will be **interesting to use.**

2. *It* as the subject of a sentence

It can tell about time or weather.

It's nine o'clock.   **It** snowed yesterday.
It will be morning soon.   **It**'s hot out.

It can also tell about an idea.
An adjective + infinitive can come after *it*.

It's **easy to drive** this car.
It wasn't **hard to push** the pedal.
It will be **interesting to use** that new computer.

Exercises

4A: *It* **as subject.** Ask and answer.

Melanie carrying an umbrella/raining
　　STUDENT A Why is Melanie carrying an umbrella?
　　STUDENT B Because it's raining.

1. they going to bed/11 o'clock
2. the girls wearing coats/snowing
3. she making lunch/almost noon
4. you going to the beach/hot out
5. he still sleeping/Saturday

4B: **Adjective + infinitive.** Make a sentence. Use Cue Book Chart 2.

steak/expensive/**1**
<u>Steak</u> is <u>expensive</u> <u>to eat</u>.

1. milk/good/**2**
2. a good cassette player/hard/**3**
3. an old tire/difficult/**4**
4. an office building/exciting/**5**
5. a giraffe/interesting/**6**

4C: **Adjective + infinitive.** Make a sentence. Use Cue Book Chart 2. Start with **5.**

hospitals/easy/**5**
<u>Hospitals</u> aren't <u>easy</u> <u>to build</u>.

1. wheels/difficult/**6**
2. old magazines/boring/**7**
3. motorcycles/dangerous/**8**
4. geography books/easy/**9**
5. new cars/hard/**10**

4D: *It* **as subject.** Ask and answer.

sail/swim
    STUDENT A Do you like to <u>sail</u>?
    STUDENT B Yes, and it's fun to <u>swim</u>, too.

1. skate/ski
2. play tennis/play basketball
3. watch TV/listen to the radio
4. study English/study French
5. go out with your friends/stay home

4E: *It* **as subject.** Make a sentence. Use Cue Book Chart 2.

expensive/**1**/in a restaurant
<u>It's expensive to eat in a restaurant</u>.

1. not safe/**2**/that water
2. important/**3**/good tires
3. not easy/**4**/an old automobile
4. difficult/**5**/roads in the mountains
5. helpful/**6**/a map
6. not boring/**7**/this science book
7. interesting/**8**/on a train
8. nice/**9**/letters to your friends
9. dangerous/**10**/without taillights
10. great/**1**/hamburgers on a picnic

4F: Adjective + infinitive. Make a new sentence.

They did the exercise easily. (easy)
The exercise was easy to do.

I couldn't pronounce the new words. (difficult)
The new words were difficult to pronounce.

1. We read that book. (interesting)
2. She couldn't start the engine. (hard)
3. He wouldn't drive that old car. (dangerous)
4. I couldn't turn the steering wheel. (difficult)
5. They couldn't open the trunk of the car. (hard)

4G: Vocabulary. Ask and answer. Use the pictures.

 /1

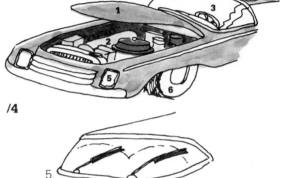

STUDENT A Did you repair the pedal?
STUDENT B Why, no. I repaired the hood.

1. 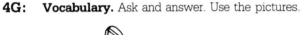 /2

2.  /3

3. 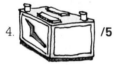 /4

4. /5

5. 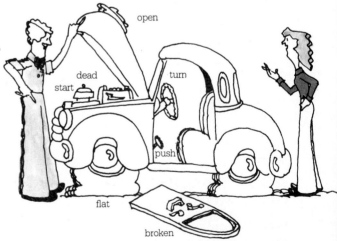 /6

COMMUNICATION PRACTICE

Guided Conversation

ATTENDANT What's the matter with your car?
DRIVER The tire is flat, and the engine
is hard to start. Can you
repair it?
ATTENDANT Well, the tire is easy to fix,
but you need a new engine.
DRIVER Oh, no! It's expensive to buy
a new engine!

open
dead
turn
start
push
flat
broken

Activities

A. Ask somebody.

Can you drive a car?
Is it more dangerous to drive in the city or in the country?
Why do you think so?

Maybe you can use . . .

good/bad roads	noisy
terrible drivers	smooth
a lot of traffic	quiet
traffic lights	dark
stop signs	rough

B. Talk with somebody.

1. You've run out of gas and you need to go to a gas station. Ask a friend for help. (Maybe he or she can take you there in a car.)

2. A driver's car won't start and the headlights don't work, so he or she calls a garage and talks to a mechanic. The driver tells the mechanic about the car and asks, "What's the matter with it? Can you fix it? When will you come?" You and another student take the parts of the driver and the mechanic and perform this conversation. (The mechanic thinks the battery is dead.)

C. What do you think?

Are women better drivers than men?
Why do you think so?

Maybe you can use . . .

safe	angry
calm	lost
brave	tired
careful	worried
helpful	excited

Self Test

Make two sentences. Follow the example.

She fixed <u>the speedometer</u>. (easy)
<u>The speedometer</u> was easy to fix.
It was easy to fix <u>the speedometer</u>.

1. They read <u>the books</u>. (boring)
2. I rode <u>that motorcycle</u>. (dangerous)
3. He repaired <u>the engine</u>. (difficult)
4. She taught <u>the English class</u>. (interesting)
5. We drank <u>that water</u>. (safe)

LESSON 5

Can you recommend a good hotel?

CONVERSATIONS

1.

LAURA   Alex, I'm bored. Let's take a vacation.

ALEX   We just took a vacation last month!

LAURA   I know. But I want to take another. I want to see mountains and deserts and rocks, but not a lot of people.

ALEX   I know just the place. Tourists seldom go there.

2.

TRAVEL AGENT   May I help you?

ALEX   Yes. We want two tickets to the moon, please.

TRAVEL AGENT   I see. And do you wish to travel first class?

ALEX   Of course. Can you recommend a good motel?

TRAVEL AGENT   Well, not right now, sir. The Lunar Motel will open in the year 2150. Perhaps you'll still want to go then.

3.

LAURA   Alex, you're funny. Tourists can't go to the moon!

ALEX   You're funny, too, Laura. You know we can't afford to go on another vacation.

LAURA   I was just joking. Let's vacation at home.

ALEX   Good idea. Home is always the best.

LAURA   Of course we'll need a new TV, and a pool, and . . .

Questions

1. What did Laura want to see? What didn't she want to see?
2. Can Alex and Laura stay at the Lunar Motel? Why?
3. Where do you and your family vacation? What do you do there?

VOCABULARY

New Words

1. **desert**

3. **moon**

sand

2. **forest**

4. **valley**

to af ford', *v.* to have the money for: *I can't afford to buy a new car this year.*

an oth'er, *pron.* one more: *This hamburger is great. I want another.*

bored, *adj.* not excited: *The boy is bored because all of his friends are out of town.*

des'ert(s), *n.* *It's very dry in a desert.* See Picture 1.

first'-class', *adj.* very good: *This is a first-class hotel.*

first' class', *adv.* in a very good way: *Do you want to travel first class?*

for'est(s), *n.* *There are a lot of trees in a forest.* See Picture 2.

fre'quent ly, *adv.* See Grammar.

to joke, *v.* to say a funny thing: *I laughed when Paul joked with the teacher.*

just, *adv.* really: *The weather today is just beautiful.*

moon(s), *n.* *I can't see the moon tonight.* See Picture 3.

mo tel'(s), *n.* a hotel for people with cars: *When we were on vacation, we stayed in a motel.*

oft'en, *adv.* See Grammar.

oth'er(s), *pron.* See Grammar.

pas'sen ger(s), *n.* a rider in a car, bus, train, or plane: *The passengers got on the bus at the corner.*

rare'ly, *adv.* See Grammar.

to rec'om mend', *v.* to tell somebody about a good thing: *She recommends that hotel because it has a good restaurant and a pool.*

rock(s), *n.* a large stone; a piece of stone: *The children sat on a big rock.*

sand, *n.* *The girls played in the sand on the beach.* See Picture 1.

sel'dom, *adv.* See Grammar.

some'times, *adv.* See Grammar.

tour'ist(s), *n.* a traveler for fun: *Many tourists visit the city in the summer.*

to trav'el, *v.* to go from one place to another: *We traveled from New York to Hong Kong by plane.*

trav'el a'gent(s), *n.* a helper for tourists: *My travel agent got my train tickets and recommended a good hotel.*

u'su al ly, *adv.* See Grammar.

to va ca'tion, *v.* to go on a vacation: *They vacationed in Spain.*

val'ley(s), *n.* a low place between mountains: *They drove from the mountains into the valley.* See Picture 4.

to wish, *v.* to want: *She wishes to interview the famous artist.*

Idioms

Do you like ice cream?
Of course!

Of course I want to see this movie.

I want a new car. **Of course,** I don't have any money . . .

take + noun
Laura **took a vacation** last month.

Word Study

afford
Use *afford* with a form of *can* or *be able to*.
Can you **afford** to take a plane?
She **wasn't able to afford** a new car.

just
I was **just** joking. (= only)
We **just** went on a vacation last month. (= not very long ago)
I know **just** the place to eat dinner. (= really, without being wrong)

wish/want
FORMAL   Do you **wish** to see a menu?
INFORMAL   What do you **want** for lunch?

ways to say *yes*

TEACHER   Will you please close the door?
STUDENT   **Yes, ma'am.** (FORMAL)

BROTHER   Close the door, please.
SISTER   **OK.** (INFORMAL)

WAITRESS   Do you wish to see a menu?
CUSTOMER   **Yes, please.** (FORMAL)

MOTHER   Do you want some ice cream?
CHILD   **Sure!** (INFORMAL)

CUSTOMER   I'd like a table by the window, please.
WAITER   **Of course, sir.** (FORMAL)

A FRIEND   Do you want to go out with me tonight?
YOU   **Of course!** (INFORMAL)

Principal Parts of Verbs

base form	present participle	past tense	past participle
af ford	af ford ing	af ford ed	af ford ed
joke	jok ing	joked	joked
rec om mend	rec om mend ing	rec om mend ed	rec om mend ed
trav el	trav el ing	trav eled	trav eled
va ca tion	va ca tion ing	va ca tioned	va ca tioned
wish	wish ing	wished	wished

Pronunciation
Sentences with Key Words BANK /b/, VERY /v/, FISH /f/, WINDOW /w/; short responses

Have you *been away?* Yes, on *vacation.*
Where did you go? *Twelve Bears Valley.*
Where did you stay? In the *forest.*
How *was* the *weather? Wonderful.*
When did you *arrive? Wednesday.*
Do you *have* to *work* this *week?*
   Yes, *Friday.*

How *was* your *vacation? Wonderful.*
Did you *travel* in the *West?* Yes,
  in *Nevada.*
Did you *have* a good time? Certainly.
Did your *family* have *fun?* Sure.
Was it *very expensive?* No.
Would you *visit* there again? Of course.

Vocabulary exercise

Choose the correct word.

afford	1. We can see the _____ at night.
first-class	2. There are a lot of _____ on this train.
forest	3. Bill is funny. He likes to _____ with his friends.
joke	4. Can you _____ a good gas station?
moon	5. He couldn't _____ to take an expensive trip.
passengers	6. He lives in a _____ between two high mountains.
recommend	7. Excuse me, sir. I _____ to buy this book.
sand	8. We drove to the _____ and looked at the trees.
valley	9. I want to stay in a _____ hotel.
wish	10. The children on the beach are making houses in the _____.

GRAMMAR

1. Frequency adverbs

Frequency adverbs answer the questions "How many times?" "How often?" "Have/Do (you) ever?" "Has/Does (she) ever?"

0%	10%	15%	30%	60%	70%	90%	100%
never	rarely	seldom	sometimes	frequently	often	usually	always

   A. Horses **never** drive automobiles.
   B. People **rarely** eat cake with soup.
   C. Students **seldom** shout in the library.
   D. Parrots **sometimes** talk.
   E. Babies **frequently** cry.
   F. Tourists **often** visit museums.
   G. Secretaries **usually** type letters.
   H. The sun is **always** hot.

2. *Another* and *the other* as pronouns

Another = one of many

Last summer we traveled from one country to another country.
Last summer we traveled from one country to another one.
Last summer we traveled from one country to **another.**

The other = one of two

There are two people on the bus.
One is the driver and the other one is a passenger.
One is the driver and **the other** is a passenger.

3. *Others/the others*

There are a lot of people in the park.
Some of them are riding bikes and **others** are walking. (= some other ones)

There are six pencils on the desk.
Four of them are yellow and **the others** are red. (= the rest)

Exercises

5A: **Frequency adverbs.** Ask and answer.

go to the movies/no/never

    STUDENT A Do you ever <u>go to the movies</u>?

    STUDENT B <u>No</u>. I <u>never</u> <u>go to the movies</u>.

1. travel by plane/yes/frequently
2. drink tea/no/never
3. joke with your friends/yes/always
4. fail tests/no/never
5. vacation at the beach/yes/usually

6. try to repair your car/no/never
7. ride your bike to school/yes/often
8. sleep late on Saturday/yes/sometimes
9. run out of gas/no/never
10. walk in the forest/no/never

5B: **Frequency adverbs.** Ask and answer.

you/borrow money/never

    STUDENT A How often <u>do you borrow</u>
                  <u>money</u>?

    STUDENT B <u>I never borrow money</u>.

he/fail tests/frequently

    STUDENT A How often <u>does he fail tests</u>?

    STUDENT B <u>He frequently fails tests</u>.

1. monkeys/wear blue jeans/rarely
2. Marion/write to Pedro/seldom
3. Lillian/fly to Bangkok/often

4. Jack/hand in his homework/always
5. Mr. and Mrs. Kim speak English/usually

5C: **Frequency adverbs.** Ask and answer.

she/vacationed in the mountains/yes/frequently

    STUDENT A <u>Has she</u> ever <u>vacationed in the mountains</u>?

    STUDENT B <u>Yes, she's frequently</u> vacationed in the mountains.

1. your brother/repaired your car/yes/often
2. they/stayed at that motel/no/never
3. she/recommended a bad hotel/yes/sometimes
4. your sisters/traveled by plane/yes/frequently
5. he/worked in a gas station/no/never

5D: ***Another* as a pronoun.** Ask and answer.

he/student/fails/course

    STUDENT A Is he a good student?

    STUDENT B No. He always fails one course or another.

1. she/travel agent/recommends/bad hotel
2. he/mailman/loses/letter
3. he/mechanic/breaks/tool
4. she/waitress/drops/dish
5. she/reporter/makes/mistake

5E: ***Another* and *the other* as pronouns.** Choose the correct word or words.

another   **the other**

1. One of my parents is a teacher; _____ is a writer.
2. There are two pies on the table. One is apple and _____ is peach.
3. My old sweater was too small, so I had to buy _____.
4. Did you eat your sandwich? Do you want _____?
5. There are two motels in this town. One is first-class, but _____ is terrible!

COMMUNICATION PRACTICE

Guided Conversation

TRAVEL AGENT May I help you?

    TOURIST Yes. I want to go to Lima.

TRAVEL AGENT All right. How do you wish to travel?

    TOURIST By plane.

TRAVEL AGENT Fine. I'll write the ticket.

    TOURIST Can you recommend a good hotel there?

TRAVEL AGENT Of course, ma'am. There's one near the airport.

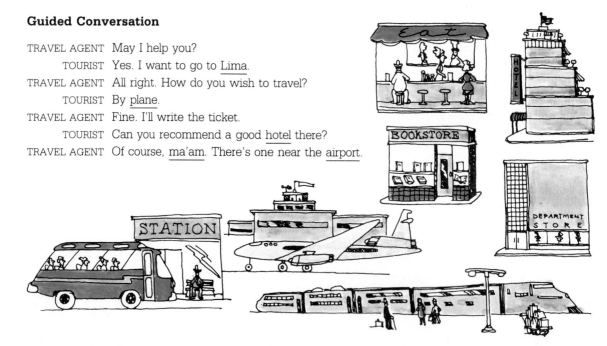

Activities

A. Ask somebody

Do you always vacation with your family?
Where do you usually go?
Do you like to travel? Why?

Maybe you can use . . .

exciting	see different places
interesting	meet new people
boring	speak another language
fun	ride trains
expensive	take planes

B. Talk with somebody

1. You're going to take a vacation. You want to stay at a first-class hotel with a pool and a good restaurant, so you talk to a travel agent about it. You and another student perform this conversation. (You can use sentences from Conversation 2.)

2. A tourist is visiting your city and wants to know more about it. The tourist stops at a gas station and asks the attendant, "Is it ever cold here? Does it often rain? Are there any good hotels? Can you recommend a good restaurant?" You and a classmate take the parts of the tourist and the attendant. (The tourist will also ask about museums, hospitals, stores, parks, beaches, and sports.)

C. What do you think?

What's the best place for a vacation—
the mountains, the beach, or the city?
Why do you think that's the best?

Maybe you can use . . .

climb	take pictures
swim	visit museums
sail	like hot weather
ski	hate crowds

Self Test

Choose the best word.

always   never   rarely   sometimes   usually

1. The sun shines seven days a week here.
   The sun _____ shines here.
2. The sun shines only one day a week here.
   The sun _____ shines here.
3. The sun shines six days a week here.
   The sun _____ shines here.
4. The sun doesn't shine on any day here.
   The sun _____ shines here.
5. The sun shines one or two days a week here.
   The sun _____ shines here.

LESSON 6

CONVERSATIONS

1.

MR. BUSH I think we're lost.

MRS. BUSH I'll turn in at this farm and ask for directions.

MR. BUSH Good idea. I want to get back to the city before dinner. Driving at night can be dangerous.

MRS. BUSH Yes, and it looks like rain.

2.

MRS. BUSH Sir, how many blocks is it to Centerville?

FARMER There aren't any blocks in the country, ma'am. You have to go back down that road for thirty-five kilometers.

MRS. BUSH Go back! Well, can I turn around here?

FARMER Sure. Just don't run into my cow!

3.

MRS. BUSH The road is awfully narrow here. Turning around won't be easy. Would you give me directions?

FARMER Sure. Just take it easy, ma'am. Back up carefully. Wait! Step on the brakes! Look out for the mud!

MRS. BUSH What did you say? Oh, no! We're stuck! What are we going to do now?

MR. BUSH Sir, would you call a taxi, please? We have to get back to Centerville.

FARMER There aren't any taxis here either. Would you like to rent my horse?

Questions

1. Where were Mr. and Mrs. Bush?
2. What kind of accident did they have?
3. Were you ever in an automobile accident?
   Were you the driver or a passenger? What happened?

VOCABULARY

New Words

1. accident
2. blocks
3. cow
calf
4. farm
farmer
wide
narrow
6. pig
piglet
7. sheep
lamb

ac′ci dent(s), *n. She was hurt in a train accident.* See Picture 1.

aw′ful ly, *adv.* very: *It's awfully cold out.*

back, *adv.* behind; the other way: *He left his book on his desk, so he had to go back and get it.*

to back′ up′, *v.* to move with the back first: *The driveway is narrow, so you'll have to back up carefully.*

block(s), *n. The library is three blocks from our school.* See Picture 2.

brake(s), *n.* a part of a car: *The car stopped when she stepped on the brakes.*

calf (calves), *n.* a baby cow: *The calf was crying for some milk.* See Picture 3.

cow(s), *n. The farmer gets milk from his cows.* See Picture 3.

to de cide′, *v.* to think about and then do something: *She decided to buy a TV.*

dirt, *n.* ground: *His plants won't grow because the dirt is too dry.*

ei′ther, *adv.* any more than: *Bill isn't going, so I won't go either.*

farm(s), *n. There are twenty horses and five cows on that farm.* See Picture 4.

farm′er(s), *n. That farmer grew a lot of corn last year.* See Picture 4.

to get to, *v.* to arrive at: *What time did you get to school?*

field(s), *n.* an open place on a farm for plants or animals: *They grow beans in that field.*

high′way(s), *n.* a big road: *Does this highway go into the city?*

kil′o me′ter(s), *n.* 1,000 meters: *It's 400,000 kilometers to the moon.*

lamb(s), *n.* a baby sheep: *Six lambs were born this spring.* See Picture 7.

like, *prep.* almost the same as: *Our house is like theirs.*

to look′ out′, *v.* to be careful: *Look out for cars when you cross the street.*

mud, *n.* wet dirt: *The children were dirty because they were playing in the mud.*

nar′row, *adj.* not far from one side to the other: *The streets in the old town were very narrow.* See Picture 5.

pig(s), *n. Do those pigs usually stand in the mud?* See Picture 6.

pig′let(s), *n.* a baby pig: *The mother pig has five piglets.* See Picture 6.

to rent, *v.* to pay money to use, but not to buy, something: *She rented a car on her vacation.*

to run′ in′to, *v.* 1. to meet: *I ran into John at the drugstore yesterday.* 2. to hit; to have an accident with: *He had to repair his car because he ran into a truck.*

sheep, (sheep) *n. There's one sheep near the fence and three sheep under the tree.* See Picture 7.

to step, *v.* to pick up the foot and put it down in a different place: *Step carefully here because there's a lot of mud.*

stuck, *adj.* not able to move; fastened: *Our car was stuck in the mud.*

to turn′ a round′, *v.* to turn and go the other way: *Centerville is north and we're going south, so we'll have to turn around to get there.*

to turn′ in′, *v.* to turn and go in: *I turned in at your house to see you.*

wide, *adj.* far from one side to the other; not narrow: *The river is very wide here.* See Picture 5.

Idioms

He's not working today.
He's **taking it easy.**

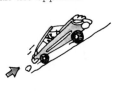

Please don't get excited, sir.
Take it easy.

step on

step on the gas = step on the gas pedal so the car will move
step on the brakes = step on the brake pedal so the car will stop
Step on it! = step on the gas so the car will go; hurry!

Word Study

up/down

Up and *down* usually mean the opposite.

The car went **up** the hill.

The car went **down** the hill.

Sometimes *up* and *down* mean the same.
The car went **up** the street. = The car went **down** the street.

Up and *down* can add to the meanings of some words.
Please **write down** your answers.
Buildings **burn down.**

Don't **back up** here.
Cars and other things **burn up.**

Use *too* after an affirmative sentence and *either* after a negative sentence.
She's going to the movies, and Jack is going, **too.**
She doesn't have a ticket, and Jack doesn't have one **either.**

two-word verb

back up   He'll **back up** the car.   OR   He'll **back** the car **up.**
He'll **back** it **up.**

Principal Parts of Verbs

base form	present participle	past tense	past participle
back up	back ing up	backed up	backed up
de cide	de cid ing	de cid ed	de cid ed
get to	get ting to	got to	got ten to
look out	look ing out	looked out	looked out
rent	rent ing	rent ed	rent ed
run in to	run ning in to	ran in to	run in to
step	step ping	stepped	stepped
turn a round	turn ing a round	turned a round	turned a round
turn in	turn ing in	turned in	turned in

Pronunciation   Sentences with Key Words BANK /b/, DESK /d/, GIRL /g/, PAGE /p/, TABLE /t/, CAR /k/; sentence stress

We **decided** to **pick up** the **pig.**
They **started** to **put** the **pigs** in **bags.**
Describe the **accident** in your **block.**
Dick stepped on the **pedal.**
We **rented** good **bikes** at the **motel.**
Back up, so you **won't** get **stuck** in the **mud.**

Greg always **bragged** about his good **brakes.**
Pat packed butter in big **tubs.**
He **stopped** the **taxi** and **stepped** into it.
She **helps** the **workmen pick up supplies.**
She **helped** them **yesterday.**
Look out for **cows** at your **picnic.**

Vocabulary Exercise

Choose the correct word.

accident	1. The car didn't stop because the _____ didn't work.
back	2. He needs to take a bath because he fell in the _____.
brakes	3. We can't turn around here because the road is too _____.
decided	4. Did she hurt her leg in the _____?
farmer	5. I forgot my glasses, so I went _____ for them.
highway	6. Mrs. Green _____ a car to drive to the country.
mud	7. The boy's feet were wet because he _____ in the river.
narrow	8. James _____ to buy a new car.
rented	9. There are a lot of signs on the side of the _____.
stepped	10. That _____ has a lot of cows and chickens.

GRAMMAR

1. *-ing* forms of verbs as nouns

The *-ing* form of a verb can be the subject of a sentence.

Driving is easy. = It's easy to drive.
Flying costs a lot of money. = It costs a lot of money to fly.
Joking with your friends is fun. = It's fun to joke with your friends.

The *-ing* form of a verb can be an object.

She doesn't recommend **staying** in that motel.
He wants to improve his **swimming,** so he practices every day.
Did they talk about **vacationing** on the moon?

2. Linking verbs + *like/different from*

Like and *different from* can follow linking verbs.

A piglet looks almost the same as a pig. A piglet **looks like** a pig.
That can't be coffee! It **smells like** tea!
What's that noise? It **sounds like** a broken engine.
Is that your granddaughter? She**'s like** her mother.

A lamb doesn't look the same as a calf. A lamb **looks different from** a calf.
Does this rock feel the same as that one? No, it **feels different from** that one.
Peaches **are different from** bananas.

It **looks like** rain. = There are clouds, so I think it will rain.

Exercises

6A: *-ing* **verbals as nouns.** Ask and answer.

fun/visiting a farm
    STUDENT A What do you think is <u>fun</u>?
    STUDENT B I think <u>visiting a farm</u> is <u>fun</u>.

1. awful/studying for a test
2. wonderful/dancing under the moon
3. boring/waiting for a bus
4. dangerous/crossing a wide river
5. difficult/driving at night

6. exciting/watching a soccer game
7. terrible/failing a course
8. silly/singing in the shower
9. important/driving carefully
10. hard/washing the dirt from my car

6B: *-ing* **verbals as nouns.** Ask and answer.

read a lot of books/important
    STUDENT A Do you like to <u>read a lot of books</u>?
    STUDENT B <u>Yes</u>, <u>reading</u> is <u>important</u>.

1. eat good food/yes/fun
2. write long letters/no/boring
3. drive to work every day/no/expensive
4. travel from one country to another/yes/exciting
5. study for tests/no/difficult

6C: *-ing* **verbals as nouns.** Change the sentence.

It's fun to play chess.
<u>Playing chess is fun.</u>

1. It's awful to have an accident.
2. It's expensive to rent a big car.
3. It isn't important to sell this car.
4. It isn't easy to turn around here.
5. It was difficult to define the word.

6. It was exciting to fly to Japan.
7. It can be boring to ride on a train.
8. It can be hard to learn to drive.
9. It can be fun to travel.
10. It will be easy to repair your brakes.

6D: *-ing* **verbals as nouns.** Ask and answer.

sail/swim
    STUDENT A Do you like <u>sailing</u>?
    STUDENT B Yes. It's fun to <u>sail</u>, but I like <u>swimming</u>, too.

1. eat/cook
2. skate/ski
3. walk/drive
4. travel/stay home
5. watch TV/go to the movies.

6E: Linking verbs + *like*. Ask and answer. Use Cue Book Chart 3.

on/**1**/10
    STUDENT A What's that <u>on</u> the <u>mountain</u>?
    STUDENT B I don't know, but it looks like a <u>cow</u>.

1. in/**2**/11	3. on/**4**/13	5. on/**6**/15	7. on/**8**/17	9. next to/**19**/**20**
2. in/**3**/12	4. near/**5**/14	6. across/**7**/16	8. on/**9**/18	10. near/**22**/**21**

6F: Frequency adverbs. Ask and answer. Use Cue Book Chart 3.

lived on/**1**/no/never
    STUDENT A Have you ever <u>lived on</u> a <u>mountain</u>?
    STUDENT B <u>No</u>, I've <u>never</u> <u>lived on</u> a <u>mountain</u>.

1. walked in/**2**/yes/often	6. sailed on/**9**/no/never
2. slept in/**3**/no/never	7. driven/**14**/yes/often
3. worked on/**4**/yes/frequently	8. ridden in/**15**/yes/frequently
4. swum in/**7**/yes/often	9. bought/**16**/no/never
5. played on/**8**/yes/frequently	10. driven/**17**/yes/often

COMMUNICATION PRACTICE

Guided Conversation

    TOURIST Excuse me. How far is it to the <u>museum</u>?
  POLICEMAN It's <u>three</u> blocks.
    TOURIST Is it <u>hard</u> to find?
  POLICEMAN Oh, no. Finding it is easy. Just walk
                down this street for <u>two blocks</u>,
                then turn to the <u>right</u> and walk
                <u>one</u> more <u>block</u>.
    TOURIST Thank you.
  POLICEMAN You're welcome.

Activities

A. Ask somebody.

How are you like your friends?
How are you different from them?

B. Talk with somebody.

1. You want to go to the post office from school. Ask a classmate for directions.

2. A reporter is doing a TV interview about living on a farm. The reporter interviews a farmer and asks, "How many animals do you have? What kind are they? What do you grow in your fields? Is it hard or easy to own a farm?" You and another student take the parts of the reporter and the farmer and perform the interview. (The reporter will also ask about the farmer's family, house, and vacations.)

C. What do you think?

How is the city different from the country?
Which one is better? Why?

Self Test

Make a new sentence. Use the *-ing* form of the verb.

1. It's easy to speak English.
2. It's expensive to go to the movies.
3. It's exciting to ride motorcycles.
4. It's terrible to have an accident.
5. It's dangerous to walk on the highway.
6. It's boring to discuss school.
7. It's hard to give good directions.
8. It's helpful to study at home.
9. It's awful to get lost.
10. It's difficult to drive at night.

LESSON 7

Cars Are Like Their Owners. Or Are They?

READING

There are many different kinds of cars in this world. My cousin thinks this is because cars are like their owners. He says, "Rich people own expensive cars, big people have large cars, and old people drive old cars." I don't think I agree with this idea.

My neighbor, Mrs. Hill, is 82 years old. She drives only on Tuesdays, and then she drives only to the bank. She seldom drives more than 30 kilometers an hour, and she never has anybody with her. You think Mrs. Hill has a very old, very small car. Right?

Wrong! Her car is brand-new*. It can hold six passengers, and it has a huge engine. It can travel up the side of a mountain at 200 kilometers an hour!

    *brand-new very new

Mr. Jackson lives next to Mrs. Hill. Mr. Jackson is fat! What kind of car does he have? You've already guessed! His car is tiny*. After a big meal, he doesn't fit behind the steering wheel. His wife has to push him into the seat*.

    *tiny very small
    *seat(s) See New Words.

My friend Diego is an artist. He paints beautiful pictures with brilliant* colors. *His* car is black! Mrs. Bates owns an ancient* car. Smoke* and steam* boil* out of the engine when she drives it. Poor Mrs. Bates. Poor? She owns four restaurants and has two million dollars* in the bank! My Uncle Joe has a tiny car. Every Sunday he drives to the country with his wife, his five children, his mother, and their dog.

    *brilliant very bright
    *ancient very old
    *smoke See New Words.
    *steam See New Words.
    *to boil See New Words.
    *dollar(s) U.S. money

Now you have read about my friends and their cars. Do you agree with my cousin?

Maybe your family has a car. Does it say something about you? Why don't you write and tell me about it? I never travel, so I have a lot of time to read letters. You see, I don't own a car.

Questions

1. What does the writer's cousin think about cars and their owners?
2. What kind of car does Mr. Jackson need? What about Uncle Joe?
3. What kind of car do you want to own? Why?

VOCABULARY

New Words

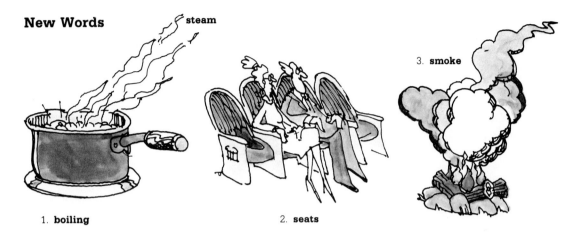

1. **boiling**   2. **seats**   3. **smoke**

to boil, *v. When the water boils, add the rice.* See Picture 1.

com′ma(s), *n.* See Reading and Writing Skills.

ex′cla ma′tion point′(s), *n.* See Reading and Writing Skills.

per′i od(s), *n.* See Reading and Writing Skills.

ques′tion mark′(s), *n.* See Reading and Writing Skills.

quo ta′tion mark′(s), *n.* See Reading and Writing Skills.

seat(s), *n. She put her purse on the seat next to her.* See Picture 2.

smoke, *n. The fire made a lot of smoke.* See Picture 3.

steam, *n. I think the water is boiling, because I can see steam.* See Picture 1.

Principal Parts of Verbs

base form	present participle	past tense	past participle
boil	boil ing	boiled	boiled

READING AND WRITING SKILLS

Punctuation

1. Period .

Use a period at the end of a sentence.

Bill speaks English**.**

2. Question mark ?

Use a question mark at the end of a question.

Does he study every day**?**

3. Comma ,

Use a comma before or after a name when somebody is talking to somebody.

Tom, do you have your geography book?

I'll be with you in a minute, Mr. Jackson.

Use a comma before and after a noun in apposition.

My neighbor, Mrs. Hill, has a huge car.

Use a comma between the words or ideas in a series.

She bought books, pencils, erasers, and pens.

Some cars are blue, some are green, and others are orange.

Use a comma when you write two sentences together with *and, but,* or *or.*

Some cars are old, and others are new.

Mr. Green is big, but his car is little.

Did you do your homework, or did you watch TV?

4. Exclamation point !

Use an exclamation point after a loud command.

Look out! Don't fall in the water!

Use an exclamation point when somebody is excited, angry, or very happy.

Mr. Jackson is as fat as an elephant!

Oh, no! We're stuck!

We won!

5. Quotation marks " "

Use quotation marks around somebody's words. Use a comma, too.

Marion asked, "Did you run into Joe at the market today?"

The mechanic said, "Your battery is dead."

When the words in quotation marks come first, use a comma, a question mark, or an exclamation point.

"I need a new tire," she said.

"Where are you going?" he asked.

"Step on the brakes!" shouted the policeman.

Exercises

7A: **Punctuation.** Write each sentence with commas. Use a period or a question mark.

They speak English French and Spanish
They speak English, French, and Spanish.

1. Mr. Cox teaches history geography math and music
2. Would you like pop lemonade tea or coffee
3. Did he buy potatoes carrots beans or peas
4. The mechanic repaired the brakes the headlights and the steering wheel
5. Some people work others study and a few people just take it easy

7B: **Punctuation.** Write each sentence with the correct punctuation. Use quotation marks.

He said People are funny
He said, "People are funny."

1. The attendant said Please open your hood
2. The policeman asked Do you have a driver's license
3. Al shouted Stop There's a cow in the road
4. Help shouted the frightened boy
5. What time does the show start asked Mrs. Bates

COMMUNICATION PRACTICE

Writing Activities

A. Does a friend, a neighbor, or somebody in your family own a car? Write three or four sentences about the person and the car. Are they alike or different? You can use sentences from the Reading.

B. Look out the window. Choose a car and write several sentences to describe it. Then write about the owner of the car. What kind of person do you think he or she is? Look at the Reading for words and ideas.

Unit Self Test

Make two sentences. Follow the example.

fun/joke with friends
It's fun to joke with friends.
Joking with friends is fun.

1. interesting/vacation in the mountains
2. terrible/fail a test
3. boring/discuss automobiles
4. easy/repair speedometers
5. exciting/drive a powerboat

Complete the sentence. Use the correct adverb.

6. Beverly fails all of her history tests.
   She _____ passes them. (often/never)
7. Joe drives to school every day.
   He _____ drives to school. (always/seldom)
8. Karen speaks English with her friends.
   She _____ speaks English. (never/often)
9. Bob saw only one movie last year.
   He _____ goes to the movies. (often/seldom)
10. David eats a lot of pears and apples.
    He _____ eats fruit. (frequently/rarely)

LESSON 8

Are you ready to order?

CONVERSATIONS

1.

WAITER   Are you ready to order?

MRS. FRY   Yes, we are. Are the lamb chops good?

WAITER   Oh, yes, ma'am. We stuff them with cabbage. Everybody loves them.

MRS. FRY   That sounds good. I'll have them.

MR. FRY   I think I'll have the shrimp. How do you cook them?

WAITER   We cook them in boiling milk and serve them with rice and vegetables. They're very good!

MR. FRY   Are the vegetables fresh?

WAITER   Oh, yes, sir! All of our food is fresh, and nothing is artificial.

2.

MRS. FRY   These lamb chops aren't very good.

MR. FRY   These shrimp are awful! And that singing waiter is worse! Who recommended this restaurant?

MRS. FRY   My boss. She likes natural food.

MR. FRY   Natural food? These shrimp taste like old tires! They don't have a cook in the kitchen—they have an automobile mechanic!

3.

MR. FRY   I don't have enough money!

MRS. FRY   Don't worry. I can use my credit card.

MR. FRY   OK. But I'm really burned up about this. The music was too loud, the food was terrible, and now I can't afford to pay the check!

MRS. FRY   Are you going to give the waiter a tip?

MR. FRY   Yes. I'm going to tell him, "Don't sing anymore!"

Questions

1. Did Mr. and Mrs. Fry like the food in the restaurant? Why?
2. Was Mr. Fry happy or angry when he got the check? Why?
3. Did you ever get terrible food in a restaurant? What did you do?

VOCABULARY

New Words

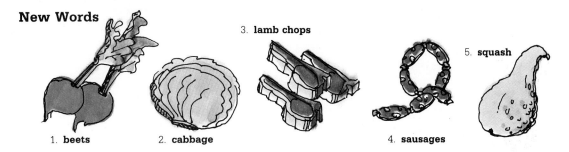

3. **lamb chops**

5. **squash**

1. **beets**   2. **cabbage**   4. **sausages**

an′y more′, *adv.* ever again: *She won't go out with Bill anymore because he's always late.*

ap′pe tiz′er(s), *n.* food to eat before the most important part of a meal: *They served appetizers before dinner.*

ar′ti fi′cial, *adj.* made from something else; not natural: *There were artificial flowers on the table.*

beef, *n.* meat from a cow: *He eats a lot of beef: steaks, hamburgers, and sandwiches.*

beet(s), *n.* a red vegetable: *She's going to boil the beets.* See Picture 1.

bev′er age(s), *n.* a drink: *Water, milk, and lemonade are beverages.*

cab′bage, *n.* a green vegetable: *You can cook cabbage or eat it in salads.* See Picture 2.

cer′e al, *n.* a hot or cold food, usually for breakfast: *Yesterday morning I had hot rice cereal with milk and fruit.*

check(s), *n.* a list with the cost of food in a restaurant. *After dinner, they paid the check.*

chop(s), *n. I had pork chops for dinner, and Lois had lamb chops.* See Picture 3.

cred′it card′(s), *n.* a card so you can pay without money: *Mr. Bach paid for his gas and oil with a credit card.*

en′tree(s), *n.* the most important food at lunch or dinner: *The entree tonight is chicken and rice.*

fresh, *adj.* just made or grown: *I just pulled the beets, so I know they're fresh.*

lamb, *n.* meat from a lamb: *I think leg of lamb is delicious.*

meat, *n.* food from the body of an animal: *Do you want meat or fish for dinner?*

nat′u ral, *adj.* growing or living in the world; not made from anything different: *I like milk and other natural beverages, but I don't like pop.*

pork, *n.* meat from a pig: *She thinks beef and veal are better than pork.*

real, *adj.* correct; natural; not artificial: *The fruit in her drawing looks almost real.*

sau′sage, *n.* meat, usually pork or veal, cut into very small pieces: *He put a lot of salt and pepper in the sausage.*

sau′sage(s), *n. Mildred likes pork sausages for breakfast.* See Picture 4.

to serve, *v.* to put (food or beverages) on the table: *The waitress served the soup.*

to spill, *v.* to make (milk, water, salt, or something like them) fall: *He spilled lemonade on his shirt.*

squash, *n. This kind of squash grows well in hot weather.* See Picture 5.

to stuff, *v.* to fill (a chicken or other food) with something: *My mother stuffed the chicken with bread and sausage.*

to swing, *v.* to move one way and then the other: *We swing our arms when we walk.*

    tip(s), *n.* 1. a small gift of money for a waiter or waitress: *The waitress was very nice, so I left her a big tip.* 2. some helpful news: *Mr. Harris gave me some tips about safe driving.*

veal, *n.* meat from a calf: *May I have another veal chop, please?*

Idiom

burned up = angry

Word Study

would like/will have

FORMAL   What **would** you **like?**
           I'd like a steak and a salad, please.

INFORMAL What**'ll** you **have?**
           I'll have a steak and a salad, please.

anymore/any more

Use *anymore* and *any more* with *not.*
She does**n't** work at that restaurant **anymore.**
I don't want another lamb chop. I ca**n't** eat **any more** (food).

real/artificial

Anna likes **real** flowers because they smell beautiful.
Mark likes **artificial** flowers because they last a long time.

natural/artificial

We ate in the **natural** light of candles.
In the **artificial** light from the lamps, the room was as bright as day.

with

With shows people or things together in some way.
She has a car **with** four seats.
Give it to the man **with** the blue sweater.
She cut her steak **with** a knife.
The boy is playing **with** his dog.
I don't like to travel **with** a crowd.
Do you want sugar **with** your tea?
He likes ice cream **with** fruit.
The sky was dark **with** clouds.
We woke up **with** the sun.
They sailed **with** the wind.

Principal Parts of Verbs

base form	present participle	past tense	past participle
serve	serv ing	served	served
spill	spill ing	spilled	spilled
stuff	stuff ing	stuffed	stuffed
swing	swing ing	swung	swung

Pronunciation

Sentences with Key Words SHE /š/, CHOOSE /č/; final rising-falling intonation

A **Shirley,** let's **finish** these **dishes.**
The **refreshments** were **delicious.**

B What did you like?

A The **shrimp** salad, the **fresh** fruit,
and the **sugar** cookies.

B I used your **special directions.**

C Look at these awful **pictures.**

D They aren't **natural.** We look like **statues.**
And look at **Charlie's chin.**

C Who **chose** the photographer?

D A good photographer **catches** you when you
aren't **watching.**

Vocabulary Exercise

Choose the correct word.

anymore	1. We had soup for an appetizer and steak for an _____.
artificial	2. After lunch, Carmen paid the _____.
beverage	3. She _____ the fish with vegetables.
check	4. I don't have any money, so I'll pay with my _____.
credit card	5. This milk tastes terrible! I don't think it's _____.
entree	6. The waitress doesn't work at that restaurant _____.
fresh	7. The waiter was very nice, so I gave him a big _____.
spilled	8. What do you want for a _____, coffee or tea?
stuffed	9. The waiter _____ the salad on the table.
tip	10. The soup is green because it has _____ color in it.

GRAMMAR

-*ing* verbals as adjectives

The *-ing* form of a verb can be an adjective.

The water is boiling. Use the **boiling** water to make tea.
The waiter was singing. The customers enjoyed the **singing** waiter.

We use this wheel to steer. Our **steering** wheel is brown.
He sleeps in that bag. His **sleeping** bag is easy to carry.

Exercises

8A: *-ing* **verbals as adjectives.** Ask and answer.

waiter/listen to/sing
> STUDENT A What kind of waiter did you listen to?
> STUDENT B I listened to a singing waiter.

1. dog/hear/bark
2. saleswoman/meet/travel
3. puppy/carry/sleep
4. water/use/boil
5. rain/feel/fall
6. building/see/burn
7. bear/watch/dance
8. lamp/sell/hang
9. door/push/swing
10. parrot/buy/talk

8B: *-ing* **verbals as adjectives.** Make a sentence.

John wants to drink, but he doesn't have a glass.
John needs a drinking glass.

1. Clara wants to read, but she doesn't have a lamp.
2. Laura wants to swim, but she doesn't have a pool.
3. Alex wants to run, but he doesn't have any shoes.
4. George wants to park, but he doesn't have a place.
5. Martha wants to draw, but she doesn't have a pen.
6. Richard wants to drive, but he doesn't have any gloves.
7. Tina wants to write, but she doesn't have any paper.
8. Bill wants to cook, but he doesn't have a spoon.
9. Linda wants to fish, but she doesn't have a boat.
10. Carlos wants to bake, but he doesn't have any pans.

8C: **With.** Ask and answer.

make/sausage/pork and veal

STUDENT A   How did you <u>make</u> the <u>sausage</u>?
STUDENT B   I <u>made</u> it with <u>pork and veal</u>.

1. serve/beef/fresh squash
2. eat/cereal/milk and sugar
3. break/window/a rock
4. stuff/lamb chops/apples
5. write/letter/a pencil

6. cook/beets/butter and salt
7. cut/steak/a knife
8. boil/shrimp/onions
9. pay/check/a credit card
10. drink/tea/sugar and lemon

8D: **-ing verbals as adjectives.** Ask and answer. Use Cue Book Chart 4.

who/sing/sound/terrible

STUDENT A   <u>Who</u> was <u>singing</u>?
STUDENT B   The <u>waiters</u>. And the <u>singing</u> waiters sounded <u>terrible</u>.

1. what/burn/smell/awful
2. who/cry/sound/unhappy
3. what/swing/look/dangerous
4. what/talk/be/too noisy
5. what/ring/sound/terrible

6. what/boil/smell/good
7. who/run/be/noisy
8. who/shout/be/angry
9. who/laugh/be/very excited
10. what/break/sound/awful

8E: **-ing verbals as adjectives.** Complete the sentence.

My aunt <u>boiled</u> the shrimp.
The <u>boiling</u> shrimp smelled delicious.

1. The baby <u>cried</u> all night.
   Her father held the _____ baby.
2. The wind <u>blew</u> the leaves into the air.
   He liked to watch the _____ leaves.
3. The passengers <u>waited</u> for the train for an hour.
   The _____ passengers were very angry.
4. The children <u>listened</u> to the story.
   The _____ children were very quiet.
5. The moon <u>shone</u> brightly last night.
   It was fun to walk under the _____ moon.

8F: *-ing* **verbals as adjectives.** Ask and answer.

wheel/steer with

    STUDENT A Do you need <u>a wheel</u> to <u>steer with</u>?

    STUDENT B Yes, I need <u>a steering wheel</u>.

water/drink

    STUDENT C Do you need <u>some water</u> to <u>drink</u>?

    STUDENT D Yes, I need <u>some drinking water</u>.

1. license/fish
2. oil/cook with
3. spoon/serve with
4. paper/type on
5. spoon/cook with

6. bag/travel with
7. paper/wrap with
8. pan/bake in
9. gloves/drive in
10. paper/write on

COMMUNICATION PRACTICE

Guided Conversation

    WAITER Would you like to order now?

  CUSTOMER Yes, please. <u>Are</u> the <u>lamb chops</u> good?

    WAITER Oh, yes. <u>They're</u> <u>delicious</u>.

  CUSTOMER All right. I'll have the <u>lamb chops with rice</u>.

    WAITER Fine. And for dessert?

  CUSTOMER I think I'll have the <u>peaches</u>.

    WAITER Very good. Would you like a beverage?

  CUSTOMER Yes. Some <u>coffee</u>, please.

MENU

ENTREES

shrimp and tomato salad
lamb chops with rice
pork and beans
veal steak with carrots

DESSERTS	BEVERAGES
peaches	milk
apple pie	coffee
orange cake	tea

Activities

A. Ask somebody.

What's your favorite food?
Do you ever eat that food in restaurants?
Do you like to eat in restaurants? Why?

B. Talk with somebody.

1. You're in a restaurant, but you're not very hungry, and you don't have much money. You want to order a small, not very expensive meal. Ask a classmate to take the part of a waiter or waitress, and talk to him or her about the restaurant's food. (Talk about the food on the menu next to the Guided Conversation. Ask, "Is this a big meal? Is it expensive? Which meal is the smallest?")

2. A customer is in an expensive restaurant. The waiter recommends the "meal of the day," but the customer doesn't want to order it without finding out, "What kind of meat is it? What kind of vegetables come with it? Do I get dessert, too? Can I pay with my credit card?" You and a classmate take the parts of the customer and the waiter. (The customer will also ask about soup, bread, a salad, and a beverage.)

C. What do you think?

Which is better—the food in restaurants or the food at home? Why?

Self Test

Choose the best answer.

1.	What do you like to play?	a. I'm afraid of falling trees.
2.	Do you have a driver's license?	b. I like guessing games.
3.	Are they going to stay in a tent?	c. He's a vacationing Canadian.
4.	Why don't you vacation in the forest?	d. No, I need another driving lesson.
5.	Who's that man with the camera?	e. I forgot to write it on my shopping list.
6.	How do you cook rice?	f. Some pens and some drawing paper.
7.	Why didn't you buy any cabbage?	g. No, they don't have any sleeping bags.
8.	Why is she so unhappy?	h. Put it in boiling water.
9.	What supplies do you need?	i. Please put them in this serving bowl.
10.	Where do you want the beets?	j. She didn't get a passing grade on her test.

LESSON 9

Broil the lamb over a hot fire.

CONVERSATIONS

1.

MRS. BAKER   I want to register for a cooking class.

SECRETARY   Fine. Do you want to learn Chinese cooking, French cooking, or Mexican cooking?

MRS. BAKER   French cooking, please.

SECRETARY   All right. Chef Pierre teaches that class. It's on Mondays and Wednesdays at 10:00.

2.

PIERRE   Today we're going to make broiled lamb. First, heat the stove.

ASSISTANT   All right. What next?

PIERRE   Mix some vanilla ice cream with the juice of one orange and two lemons.

ASSISTANT   Will you put that on the lamb!?!?

PIERRE   Of course not! I'll drink it! Cooking makes me thirsty!

ASSISTANT   Pierre, what will we do with the lamb?

PIERRE   Slice it and serve it with baked potatoes.

ASSISTANT   But we haven't cooked it yet!

PIERRE   Oh, yes. Broil the lamb over a hot fire with oil and garlic. Watch.

ASSISTANT   Pierre! Look out! You left your drink on the stove and it's boiling over!

PIERRE   Wonderful! This is my greatest recipe! Hot lemon-orange-ice-cream drink!

3.

MR. BAKER   How was the French cooking class?

MRS. BAKER   Not very good. Chef Pierre is very forgetful.

MR. BAKER   What happened?

MRS. BAKER   First he served the lamb without cooking it, and then he put vinegar on it instead of oil. I think I'll take Chinese cooking instead.

Questions

1. What did Mrs. Baker want to learn?
2. Did Mrs. Baker like the cooking class? Why?
3. Have you ever been unhappy with a course? Why didn't you like it?

VOCABULARY

New Words

1. **garlic**
2. **grapefruit**
3. **juice**
4. **oven**
5. **raspberries**
6. **strawberries**
7. **vinegar**

to bake, *v.* to cook in an oven: *Put the potatoes in the oven and bake them for an hour.*

to boil′ o′ver, *v.* to boil and go over the side of the pot: *The stove was too hot so the water boiled over.*

to broil, *v.* to cook over a fire: *He broiled the hamburgers on the grill.*

  chef(s), *n.* a cook: *The chef stuffed the lamb with rice and vegetables.*

  choc′o late, *n.* a sweet brown food or drink: *She always drinks hot chocolate in the morning. adj.* made with chocolate: *chocolate ice cream; chocolate cake.*

to cool, *v.* to make colder: *She used ice to cool the lemonade.*

  for get′ful, *adj.* forgetting a lot of things: *The forgetful boy left his glasses on the bus, his jacket in the library, and his book in the park.*

to fry, *v.* to cook in hot oil or butter: *I fried the steak with butter and garlic.*

  gar′lic, *n. She put a lot of garlic in the salad.* See Picture 1.

  grape′fruit, *n. We always drink grapefruit juice before dinner.* See Picture 2.

to heat, *v.* to make something hotter: *Let's heat the soup in this pot.*

  in′stant, *adj.* not needing cooking or mixing: *Do you like instant coffee?*

in stead', *adv.* in another's place: *Her sister couldn't go, so she went instead.*

in stead' of, *prep.* in the place of: *Instead of studying, he watched TV.*

juice, *n. Mark didn't drink his orange juice.* See Picture 3.

to mix, *v.* to put different things together: *You mix butter, sugar, and milk to make this dessert.*

ov'en(s), *n. She baked the bread in the oven.* See Picture 4.

rasp'ber ry (raspberries), *n. We ate all of the raspberries on those bushes.* See Picture 5.

rec'i pe(s), *n.* directions for cooking something: *Her recipe for chicken and rice sounds delicious.*

to roast, *v.* to cook meat in an oven: *The cook roasted the lamb for three hours.*

roast, *adj.* roasted: *Do you like roast beef?*

to slice, *v.* to cut into thin pieces: *Marion sliced the tomatoes and I sliced the cheese.*

sour, *adj.* tasting like lemons or vinegar: *The lemonade was too sour, so she added some sugar.*

straw'ber ry (strawberries), *n. She likes strawberries on her ice cream.* See Picture 6.

sweet, *adj.* tasting like sugar: *Cake and pie are sweet desserts.*

va nil'la, *n.* something to make food sweet: *Did you put vanilla in the cake?* *adj.* made with vanilla: *Vanilla ice cream is usually white.*

vin'e gar, *n. Do you want oil and vinegar on your salad?* See Picture 7.

Idioms

Do you like salt in your tea?
Of course I don't.
Of course not.

What next? { = What will happen next?
= What will we do next?

Word Study

transitive and intransitive verbs

She**'s boiling** the water.
The water **is boiling.**

We**'re cooling** the dessert.
The dessert **is cooling.**

She**'s heating** the rolls.
The rolls **are heating.**

He**'s baking** the bread.
The bread **is baking.**

She**'s frying** the eggs.
The eggs **are frying.**

I**'m broiling** the steaks.
The steaks **are broiling.**

He**'s roasting** the lamb.
The lamb **is roasting.**

instead of/instead

I'll learn Mexican cooking **instead of** French cooking.
I don't like French cooking. I'll learn Mexican cooking **instead.**

Principal Parts of Verbs

base form	present participle	past tense	past participle
bake	bak ing	baked	baked
boil o ver	boil ing o ver	boiled o ver	boiled o ver
broil	broil ing	broiled	broiled
cool	cool ing	cooled	cooled
fry	fry ing	fried	fried
heat	heat ing	heat ed	heat ed
mix	mix ing	mixed	mixed
roast	roast ing	roast ed	roast ed
slice	slic ing	sliced	sliced

Pronunciation   Sentences with Key Word JANE /ǰ/; past tense verb endings /d/t/əd/; final rising-falling intonation

A **Janet,** what did you learn in **college?**

B **German, Japanese,** and cooking.

A What did you cook?

B I **roasted sausages** and **boiled** a **cabbage.**
I **sliced oranges** and **mixed vegetables.**
I **heated** and **cooled** a lot of **beverages.**

C **Joe graduated** in **June** and **changed** his **job.**

D What's he doing now?

C He's **just** driving a bus.

D Who are his **passengers?**

C Some are **teen-agers** in blue **jeans.**
Others are adults with **huge packages.**

Vocabulary Exercise

Choose the correct word.

boiling over	1. Before dinner, Dave _____ the rolls in the oven.
broil	2. Miss Judge always loses things because she's so _____.
cool	3. Make a fire in the grill to _____ the steaks.
egg	4. The food was awful because he didn't follow the _____.
forgetful	5. Put the melons on ice to _____ them.
heated	6. Turn off the stove! The soup is _____!
oven	7. Do you want your _____ boiled or fried?
raspberries	8. The children ate six baskets of _____.
recipe	9. She likes _____ ice cream with strawberries.
vanilla	10. I'm going to bake a cake, so I'll heat the _____.

GRAMMAR

1. Past participles as adjectives

The past participles of many verbs can be adjectives.
You can find past participles in the Grammar Summary at the back of this book.

Lillian has baked the potatoes for dinner.
She's going to serve **baked** potatoes with cheese.

Have you ever rented a car?
We drove a **rented** car to Paris last year.

I've never broken my leg.
Bill's **broken** leg hurts.

2. *Make* + noun or object pronoun + adjective

Tom gets tired when he runs.
Running **makes Tom tired.**

We got thirsty because the sun was hot.
The hot sun **made us thirsty.**

She'll be happy when she gets this present.
This present **will make her happy.**

Exercises

9A: **Past participles as adjectives.** Ask and answer.

eat/baked potato
STUDENT A What did you eat?
STUDENT B I ate a baked potato.

1. find/broken bracelet
2. serve/stuffed chicken
3. slice/broiled steak
4. wear/torn shirt
5. drive/rented car

9B: **Past participles as adjectives.** Complete the sentence.

Joe will <u>collect</u> the papers.
He'll put the <u>collected</u> papers on the desk.

1. The cook wants to <u>improve</u> the recipe.
   She'll use the _____ recipe in her cooking class.
2. Jerry <u>stuffed</u> the cabbage with rice.
   He served the _____ cabbage for dinner.
3. David went to the gym to <u>register</u> for school.
   Now he's a _____ student.
4. Let's <u>fry</u> the potatoes.
   We'll eat the _____ potatoes with salt and pepper.
5. Will you <u>slice</u> the beets, please?
   We'll serve the _____ beets with vinegar.

9C: **Past participles as adjectives.** Complete the sentence.

Please <u>write</u> the directions for me.
I'll keep the <u>written</u> directions in my pocket.

1. The leaves <u>fell</u> during the storm.
   We put the _____ leaves in a basket.
2. Anna <u>cut</u> her finger with a knife.
   She washed her _____ finger in warm water.
3. I <u>hid</u> the gifts in the closet.
   Tommy found the _____ gifts this morning.
4. Joe <u>swept</u> the porch this morning.
   The _____ porch looks very nice.
5. I <u>tore</u> my shirt.
   Can you fix my _____ shirt for me?

9D: ***Make* + object pronoun + adjective.** Ask and answer. Use Cue Book Chart 1.

2/hot weather/no/thirsty
    STUDENT A Do <u>you</u> like <u>hot weather</u>?
    STUDENT B <u>No,</u> <u>hot weather</u> <u>makes</u> me <u>thirsty</u>.

1. **3**/vanilla ice cream/no/sick
2. **4**/funny movies/yes/happy
3. **6**/cold appetizers/yes/hungry
4. **7**/raspberries and cream/no/fat
5. **2**/working/no/tired

9E: **Past participles as adjectives.** Ask and answer. Use Cue Book Chart 4.

break/see
> STUDENT A Did somebody <u>break</u> the <u>dishes</u>?
> STUDENT B Yes. I <u>saw</u> the <u>broken</u> <u>dishes</u>.

1. burn/smell
2. spill/sit on
3. slice/find
4. tear/pick up
5. fry/eat

9F: **Vocabulary.** Ask and answer. Use Cue Book Chart 5.

an appetizer
> STUDENT A Would you like <u>an appetizer</u>?
> STUDENT B Yes, I'll have the <u>grapefruit</u>, please.

1. some soup
2. an entree
3. a vegetable
4. a cold plate
5. some dessert

COMMUNICATION PRACTICE

Guided Conversation

> WAITER Would you like an appetizer or some soup?
> CUSTOMER <u>Onion soup</u>, please.
> WAITER All right. And for an entree?
> CUSTOMER Is the <u>fish</u> good?
> WAITER Oh, yes. The <u>broiled</u> <u>fish</u> is delicious.
> CUSTOMER Fine. I'll have that. And I'll have <u>baked potatoes</u> with <u>it</u>.
> WAITER Would you like a beverage?
> CUSTOMER Yes, <u>coffee</u>, please.
> WAITER Very good. Thank you.

Activities

A. Ask somebody.

What makes you happy?

What makes you angry?

B. Talk with somebody.

1. You want to cook a delicious meal. Ask a friend to help you. Ask, ''Do you know a good recipe? What will I have to buy? How do you cook it? How many people does it serve?'' You'll also want to ask your friend for help with the work.

2. Two students are planning the menu for a class picnic. Ten people will go. Three people like hamburgers. Six people like hot dogs. Everybody but one person likes fried chicken, and that person doesn't eat any meat. (The person likes cheese and eggs.) You and another student make a shopping list for the picnic. What are you going to buy? (Don't forget bread or rolls, a salad or vegetables, and a beverage.)

C. What do you think?

Read each sentence about food. Do you think it's true or false?

1. Eating potatoes makes you fat.
2. Eating fish makes you smart.
3. Eat carrots and you'll see well at night.
4. Eat an apple every day and you'll never get sick.
5. Fruits and vegetables are better for you than meat.

Self Test

Complete the sentence. Use a past participle and a noun.

Did you tear your shirt? Yes, and I can't wear a _torn_ _shirt_ .

1. Will you boil the potatoes? Yes, I like _____ _____.
2. Did she bake the fish? No, she doesn't like _____ _____.
3. Who'll broil the lamb chops? Linda makes good _____ _____.
4. Did you write the recipe? Yes, I need a _____ _____.
5. Are you going to stuff the squash? Yes, _____ _____ is delicious.
6. Will he fry the rice? No, he hates _____ _____.
7. Let's mix these vegetables. I like _____ _____.
8. Did you break the eggs? Yes, and I stepped in the _____ _____.
9. I'll cook the cabbage. Tom likes _____ _____.
10. Please slice the ham. We'll put _____ _____ in the sandwiches.

LESSON 10

He Had to Eat His Words*

*had to eat (his) words was sorry (he) said something

READING

Since* food is important to everybody, people talk about it a lot*; but did you know that you can use food words to say almost anything?

Many English idioms* use food words. For example*, when something is easy to do, you can say, "It's *a piece of cake*." Or you can say, "It's *like taking candy* from a baby*."

Food idioms can tell about liking something or somebody very much. A proud mother points to her child and says, "She's *the apple of my eye*." Food idioms can also* tell about not liking something. A lazy* person says, "Working is *not my cup of tea*."

Did you ever hear anyone* say, "I'll *take that with a grain* of salt*"? Did he mean, "Give me some salt from the shaker*"? No. He meant, "I don't really believe that." Another person says, "My friend is *the salt of the earth*." She means, "My friend is good and friendly and helpful."

A lot of slang expressions* use food words, too. *Bread* is a slang expression for money. Very little money is *chicken feed*. When a person says, "Painting is my *bread and butter*," she means, "I paint to get the money to live."

The most important person in a place can be *the top banana* or *the big cheese*. A person of no importance* is *small potatoes*. Does somebody want a lot of attention*? He's a *hot dog*. And a terrible actor is a *ham*.

Many English idioms and slang expressions use cooking words, too. An angry person is *burned up, boiling,* or *steaming*. He needs time to *cool down*. When you're in trouble*, you're *in hot water*. When you go from a bad thing, like not seeing a stop sign, to a worse thing, like running into a police car, you go *out of the frying pan into the fire*.

*since See New Words.

*a lot often

*idiom(s) See New Words.
*example(s) one thing to explain other things. See Idioms.
*candy See New Words.

*also See New Words.

*lazy See New Words.

*anyone See New Words.
*grain(s) a very small piece
*shaker(s) See New Words.

*slang expression(s) informal way of saying something
*feed food

*importance being important
*attention being looked at and listened to

*to steam to make steam

*trouble a bad thing. See Idioms.

Questions

1. Do you think learning English is a piece of cake?
2. Have you ever gone out of the frying pan into the fire? What happened?
3. Do you know any food idioms or slang expressions in your language? What do they mean in English?

VOCABULARY

New Words

1. **candy**

2. **shakers**

al′so, *adv.* too: *Amy also ordered a hamburger.*

an′y one, *pron.* anybody: *Did anyone fail English?*

can′dy, *n. Don't give the baby any candy before dinner.* See Picture 1.

eve′ry one, *pron.* everybody: *Everyone liked the dessert.*

id′i om(s), *n.* a phrase with a meaning different from the meaning of its words: *Burned up is an idiom for "angry."*

to in clude′, *v.* to put things into; to add to: *The price of the meal includes dessert and a beverage.*

to in dent′, *v.* to write the first line of a paragraph to the right of all the other lines: *Don't forget to indent in your letter.*

la′zy, *adj.* not liking or wanting to work: *He never studies because he's too lazy.*

no′ one, *pron.* nobody: *I went to the movies because no one wanted to play ball.*

shak′er(s), *n. Please put the salt and pepper shakers on the counter.* See Picture 2.

since, *conj.* because: *Since you're tired, go to bed.*

some′one, *pron.* somebody: *Someone took my pencil.*

Idioms

Oh, no! We're **in trouble** now!

My uncles are terrible drivers.
For example, my Uncle Al had six accidents last year.

Word Study

way

We're on our **way** to the stadium.
Different foods are good for you in different **ways.**
They answered the questions in a nervous **way.**

verbs + *up* and *down*

Remember—*up* and *down* don't always tell which way.

Please **stand up.**	Don't **sit down.**
He **picked up** his books.	Please **put down** your pencils.
Hurry up!	**Slow down!**
My homework fell in the stove and **burned up.**	Our school **burned down** yesterday.
He's going to **heat up** the stove.	She waited for her coffee to **cool down.**
Can I **back up** here?	Please **write down** your answers.

Principal Parts of Verbs

base form	present participle	past tense	past participle
in clude	in clud ing	in clud ed	in clud ed
in dent	in dent ing	in dent ed	in dent ed

READING AND WRITING SKILLS

Paragraphs

A paragraph is a group of sentences about one idea. Always begin the first sentence of a paragraph on a new line and indent it.

One sentence in a paragraph usually gives the most important idea of the paragraph. This is frequently, but not always, the first sentence in the paragraph.

Exercises

10A: Paragraphs.

1. How many paragraphs are there in the article "He Had to Eat His Words"? What is the most important idea in the second paragraph? Which sentence tells this idea?

2. How many paragraphs are there in the article "Cars Are Like Their Owners. Or Are They?" (page 50) What is the most important idea in the second paragraph? Which sentence tells this idea?

10B: Paragraphs. Write each group of sentences as a paragraph. Indent the first sentence of each paragraph. Draw a line under the most important idea.

1. Learning English is hard. Yesterday morning I walked into my English class and said, "Good night, everybody." Everyone laughed but the teacher. I'm afraid I'm going to fail.

2. Slang expressions can be fun to use. They make talking to your family and friends interesting and funny, but they're very informal. It's not smart to say them to your boss or your teacher!

3. Different foods are good for you in different ways. For example, carrots are good for the eyes. Everybody knows this is true because rabbits eat carrots, and rabbits never have to wear glasses.

10C: **Paragraphs.** Look at Cue Book Chart 4. Write a paragraph of five sentences about the picture. Start with *Yesterday I went to a restaurant with my family.*

COMMUNICATION PRACTICE

Writing Activities

A. "Some people eat to live; others live to eat."
Which kind of person are you?
Write a paragraph about you and food.

Maybe you can use . . .

hate/love to cook
like the same food/new foods
boring   fun
fat   exciting
expensive   interesting

B. Think of an idiom or slang expression in your language. When do you say that expression? Do you say it when you're happy, sad, angry, or afraid? Who do you say it to? How do you say the same idea in English? (Ask your teacher for help.) Write a paragraph to answer these questions.

Unit Self Test

Choose the correct word to complete each sentence.

barking	**cut**	**heated**	**sliced**	**typed**
boiling	**falling**	**lost**	**swinging**	**winning**

1. To bake a cake, put it in a _____ oven.
2. It feels good to walk in the _____ rain.
3. Let's make sandwiches with _____ lamb and lettuce.
4. Drop the shrimp into _____ water.
5. The _____ team got a prize.
6. The kitchen is just through that _____ door.
7. Everyone in town was looking for the _____ children.
8. _____ letters are easier to read than letters in handwriting.
9. Were you afraid of the _____ dogs?
10. She put a bowl of _____ flowers on the table.

LESSON 11

My finger hurts.

CONVERSATIONS

1.

RECEPTIONIST Can I help you, sir?

PATIENT Yes. I want to see the doctor. I was playing ball, and I hurt myself.

RECEPTIONIST I see. Do you have an appointment?

PATIENT An appointment!?!? This is an emergency! I think I have a broken bone!

2.

NURSE I have a few questions for you. Have you ever had an operation?

PATIENT No, I haven't.

NURSE Have you ever had the flu?

PATIENT Yes, I had the flu last winter.

NURSE How often do you catch a cold?

PATIENT Nurse, I'm in terrible pain!

NURSE All right. You can get undressed now.

PATIENT Undressed!?!? Why do I have to get undressed? My finger hurts!

3.

DOCTOR Open your mouth and say, "Ahhhhhhh."

PATIENT Doctor, my throat doesn't hurt. My *finger* hurts! Look. I think it's broken.

DOCTOR Let's see. Yes, it's broken all right.

PATIENT Will you put it in a cast?

DOCTOR No, I'll just put a bandage around it. And I'll give you some medicine for the pain.

PATIENT Oh, thank you, Doctor. I feel better already!

Questions

1. Why did the patient go to the doctor?
2. What is the doctor going to do for the patient?
3. Have you ever had a broken bone? What happened?

VOCABULARY

New Words

1. **bandage**
2. **bones**
3. **cast**
4. **coughing**

5. His leg hurts.
   He has a **sore** leg.
   He has a **pain** in his leg.

6. **sling**

7. **sneezing**

8. She has a ribbon around her **throat.**

He's looking at her **throat.**

band′age(s), *n. She put a bandage on the boy's cut finger. See Picture 1.*

bone(s), *n. My dog found a bone in the garden. See Picture 2.*

by, *prep. See Grammar.*

cast(s), *n. The doctor put a cast on her broken leg. See Picture 3.*

cold(s), *n.* being sick and having a sore throat and nose, often with coughing and sneezing: *Brenda didn't come to school today because she has a bad cold.*

to cough, *v. The baby coughed all night because she has a cold. See Picture 4.*

else, *adj.* 1. other; different: *Will somebody else speak?* 2. more: *What else do you want?*

e mer′gen cy (emergencies), *n.* a time when you have to do something right away: *I keep a box of tools in my car to use in an emergency.*

flu, *n.* being sick, almost like having a cold, but usually not with sneezing: *Carlo stayed in bed because he had the flu.*

to get′ dressed′, *v.* to put clothes on: *I get dressed at 8:00.*

to get′ un dressed′, *v.* to take clothes off: *The patient got undressed.*

her self′, *pron. See Grammar.*

him self′, *pron. See Grammar.*

it self′, *pron. See Grammar.*

med′i cine, *n.* something to make sick people better: *Take this medicine every night.*

my self′, *pron.* See Grammar.

op′e ra′tion(s), *n.* cutting and other things done to a patient: *His knee felt better after the operation.*

our selves′, *pron.* See Grammar.

pain(s), *n.* a hurting: *Larry fell off his bike, and now he has a pain in his elbow.* See Picture 5.

pa′tient(s), *n.* a person seeing a doctor: *Dr. White saw six patients today.*

re cep′tion ist(s), *n.* a person with the job of answering the phone and meeting people in an office or company: *My cousin is the receptionist in a newspaper office.*

sling(s), *n.* *Joe's arm is sore, so he has it in a sling.* See Picture 6.

to sneeze, *v.* *I sneezed when I smelled the pepper.* See Picture 7.

sore, *adj.* hurting: *Her back hurts and her leg is sore.* See Picture 5.

them selves′, *pron.* See Grammar.

throat(s), *n.* 1. the front of the neck: *She tied a ribbon around her throat.* 2. the inside of the neck: *Open your mouth so I can look at your throat.* See Picture 8.

your self′, *pron.* See Grammar.

your selves′, *pron.* See Grammar.

Idioms

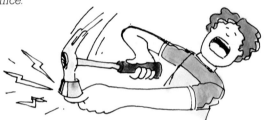

He shouted because he was **in pain.**

to catch a cold = to begin to have a cold

Word Study

flu/cold

Use *the* with *flu.* Use *a* with *cold.*
Did you have **the flu** last week?
No, I had **a cold.**

You can use an adjective with *cold,* but not with *flu.*
He has **a bad cold.**

all right

All right shows agreeing in some way.
Please give me that book.
All right. (= I agree to give it to you.)

Sir, I'm in a hurry!
All right, ma'am. I'll wait on you now. (= I understand.)

I think my arm is broken.
It's broken **all right.** (= I agree that it's broken)

transitive and intransitive verbs

I **hurt** my finger. He **grows** corn on his farm.
My finger **hurts.** Corn **grows** in that field.

***else* after pronouns**

Else can come after *somebody, anybody, something, anything, nobody,* and *nothing.*
Did **anybody else** arrive late?
There's **nothing else** in the box.

Principal Parts of Verbs

base form	present participle	past tense	past participle
get dressed	get ting dressed	got dressed	got ten dressed
get un dressed	get ting un dressed	got un dressed	got ten un dressed
cough	cough ing	coughed	coughed
sneeze	sneez ing	sneezed	sneezed

Pronunciation   Sentences with final rising intonation; noun plural endings /s/z/əz/

MAN Are the *doctors* in their *offices?*
NURSE Are you *patients?*
  Do you want to see a doctor?
MAN Will a doctor see us now?
NURSE Have you had any *operations?*
MAN Can we tell him that *ourselves?*

NURSE Have your children had the flu?
MAN Can they explain that *themselves?*
NURSE Have you broken any *bones?*
MAN Can't I tell the doctor myself?
  Won't the doctor see us now?
NURSE Will you step into his office?

Vocabulary Exercise

Choose the correct word.

bone
else
emergency
pain
patients
receptionist
sling
sneezing
sore
throat

1. The _____ called my name and told me to go into the office.
2. Jerry can't play ball because his arm is in a _____.
3. He's _____ because he has a cold.
4. Mildred doesn't want anything _____.
5. Caroline fell down and broke a _____ in her foot.
6. Try to stay calm in an _____.
7. There were three _____ in the doctor's office.
8. Joe can't run because he has a _____ leg.
9. I went to the doctor because I had a _____ in my shoulder.
10. She opened her mouth so the doctor could look at her _____.

GRAMMAR

Reflexive pronouns

Reflexive pronouns tell about the subject of a sentence.
They can be the objects of verbs or of prepositions.

I cut **myself** with a knife.
Did you hurt **yourself** yesterday?
He looked at **himself** in a mirror.
She made a sweater for **herself.**
The dog bit **itself** on the leg.

We heard **ourselves** on the tape.
Have you ever seen **yourselves** on TV?
Were they talking to **themselves?**

Reflexive pronouns can mean "without any help." Sometimes they come after *by.*

I did it **myself.** = I did it **by myself.** = I did it without any help.

Exercises

11A: **Reflexive pronouns.** Complete the sentence. Use a reflexive pronoun.

1. He told _____ to be careful.
2. They saw _____ in the mirror.
3. I burned _____ on the hot stove.
4. We bought _____ a new car.
5. Have you and Greta ever heard _____ on tape?
6. Lou and Betty taught _____ to speak English.
7. The elephant washed _____ in the river.
8. All the animals hid _____ during the storm.
9. Bill, did you hurt _____ when you fell?
10. Did you and Jack see _____ on TV?

11B: **Reflexive pronouns.** Complete the sentence. Use a reflexive pronoun.

1. Mr. Collins always talks to _____.
2. Did you and Lisa broil steaks for _____?
3. He got dressed by _____.
4. Carl put the blanket around _____.
5. She likes to look at _____ in a mirror.

11C: **Reflexive pronouns.** Ask and answer. Use Cue Book Chart 1.

2/boat/build

    STUDENT A Did you buy that boat?

    STUDENT B No, I built it myself.

1. **3**/doghouse/build
2. **4**/cake/bake
3. **6**/plant/grow
4. **7**/sweater/make
5. **2**/picture/draw

6. **3**/hamburger/broil
7. **4**/salad/fix
8. **6**/picture/paint
9. **7**/photograph/took
10. **2**/meal/cook

11D: **-ing verbals as nouns.** Ask and answer.

swim/yes/fun

    STUDENT A Do you like to swim?

    STUDENT B Yes, swimming is fun.

1. sneeze/no/terrible
2. wear a cast/no/awful
3. travel/yes/exciting
4. vacation at home/no/boring
5. catch a cold/no/awful

6. broil hamburgers/yes/fun
7. read recipes/yes/interesting
8. buy medicine/no/expensive
9. have the flu/no/terrible
10. drive/yes/terrific

11E: **-ing verbals as adjectives.** Ask and answer. Use Cue Book Chart 4.

ring

    STUDENT A Did the phone ring?

    STUDENT B Yes, and I hate ringing phones.

1. cry
2. shout

3. swing
4. sing

5. talk

11F: **Past participles as adjectives.** Ask and answer. Use Cue Book Chart 4.

waitress/break

    STUDENT A Did the waitress break the dishes?

    STUDENT B Yes, there were broken dishes on the floor.

1. chef/burn
2. customer/spill

3. chef/slice
4. boy/tear

5. anybody/fry

11G: Past participles as adjectives. Ask and answer. Use Cue Book Chart 5.

shrimp
  STUDENT A Would you like some shrimp?
  STUDENT B Yes, I'd like some boiled shrimp, please.

1. fish   3. potatoes   5. beef
2. chicken   4. tomato

COMMUNICATION PRACTICE

Guided Conversation

RECEPTIONIST Dr. Paine's office.
    PATIENT I'd like to make an appointment to see Dr. Paine.
RECEPTIONIST Certainly, ma'am. Is this an emergency?
    PATIENT Well, my leg is sore. It hurts when I walk.
RECEPTIONIST I see. Can you come in at three o'clock on Thursday?
    PATIENT Yes, I can.
RECEPTIONIST Fine.

Activities

A. Ask somebody.

Have you seen a doctor this year?
What was the matter with you?
What did the doctor do?

B. Talk with somebody.

1. You go to the doctor's office because you think your toe is broken. You don't have an appointment, so you talk to the receptionist. You and another student perform this conversation. (You can use sentences from Conversation 1.)

2. Your brother fell down the stairs and hurt his leg. You call a doctor and explain this emergency. Ask another student to take the part of the doctor and perform the conversation with you. The doctor will ask, "How old is he? When did he fall? Can he stand up? Can he walk? Can you bring him to the hospital? How will you get here?"

C. What do you think?

Who do you call in an emergency? Why?

Self Test

Complete the sentence with the correct reflexive pronoun.

1. I got dressed by _____.
2. Did they hurt _____ in the accident?
3. We made _____ a delicious meal.
4. She served _____ a dish of vanilla ice cream.
5. The puppy can't open the door by _____.
6. Marie bought _____ a motorcycle.
7. Keith, did you fix the clock _____?
8. Frank wrapped _____ in a blanket.
9. Did you and Michael teach _____ to speak French?
10. The silly dog bit _____!

LESSON 12

I'm sorry to hear that.

CONVERSATIONS

1.

DOCTOR WISE All-City Clinic. Dr. Wise speaking.

MR. POUND Hello, Doctor. This is Harold Pound.
I feel awful. My head hurts, and I have a terrible stomach ache.

DOCTOR WISE That's too bad. When did you get sick?

MR. POUND During the night. I didn't sleep at all.

DOCTOR WISE What did you have for dinner?

MR. POUND Let's see. I went to a party. We had hamburgers, garlic sausage, fried shrimp, potato chips, stuffed cabbage, . . . Oh, I had some chocolate cake, too, and some strawberry ice cream.

DOCTOR WISE I see. Well, Mr. Pound, I'll call the drugstore and give them a prescription for you. Can somebody pick it up?

MR. POUND Yes, the woman living next door will.

DOCTOR WISE Fine. Take two pills every four hours. You'll feel better in a little while.

MR. POUND I hope so.

2.

DOCTOR CROWN Good morning, Mrs. Root. What's the matter?

MRS. ROOT Oh, Doctor, I have a terrible toothache!

DOCTOR CROWN I'm sorry to hear that. Which one is it?

MRS. ROOT The one in the back. On the right.

DOCTOR CROWN Well, let me see it. Open wide, please. Yes, there's a cavity in one of your lower teeth. I'll have to fill it.

MRS. ROOT Do you have to drill?

DOCTOR CROWN Why, yes. You have to drill a cavity to fix it. But don't worry. I'll give you some medicine so it won't hurt. You won't feel a thing.

Questions

1. Why did Mr. Pound call the doctor? What did the doctor do?
2. Why did Mrs. Root go to the dentist? What will the dentist do?
3. Has a dentist ever drilled one of your teeth? What happened?

VOCABULARY

New Words

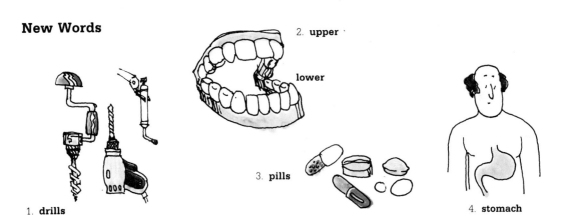

2. **upper**

lower

3. **pills**

1. **drills**

4. **stomach**

to ache, *v.* to have a pain; to hurt; to be
sore: *My back aches.*

   ache(s), *n.* a pain: *I ate too much candy,
and I got a stomach ache.*

   back′ache′(s), *n.* a pain in the back: *She
carried the heavy boxes, and now she
has a backache.*

   bet′ter, *adj.* not so sick; well: *Tom took
his medicine, and he soon got better.*

   cav′i ty (cavities), *n.* a hole: *Eating too
much sugar can make cavities in your
teeth.*

   clin′ic(s), *n.* a place to see a doctor or a
dentist, usually smaller than a hospital:
Six doctors work at that clinic.

   den′tal, *adj.* having to do with teeth or
dentists: *My dentist works at the dental
clinic on Main Street.*

   drill(s), *n.* *The dentist used a drill to fix
Ellen's teeth.* See Picture 1.

to drill, *v.* to use a drill: *The workmen are
drilling for oil.*

to fill, *v.* to give the ordered thing: *The
woman in the drugstore filled my
prescription.*

   head′ache′(s), *n.* a pain in the head: *He
took some medicine for his headache.*

to hope, *v.* to want, to wish: *I hope I pass
the history test.*

   low′er, *adj.* toward the bottom: *The
dentist looked at Kevin's lower teeth.*
See Picture 2.

   pill(s), *n.* *Take two pills every hour.* See
Picture 3.

   pre scrip′tion(s), *n.* writing from a doctor
to order medicine: *Anna's doctor gave
her a prescription for her cold.*

   prob′a bly, *adv.* maybe; almost certainly:
It's cloudy, so it will probably rain.

to re turn′, *v.* 1. to go or come back: *When Amy was in college, she returned home every weekend.* 2. to take back; to give back; to send back; to pay back; to put back: *Please return this book to the library.*

   skin, *n.* the outside of a body: *My skin got red from the sun.*

   stom′ach(s), *n. The ball hit me in the stomach. His stomach hurts because he ate too many hot dogs.* See Picture 4.

tooth′ache′(s), *n.* a pain in a tooth: *He went to the dentist because he had a toothache.*

up′per, *adj.* toward the top: *Her apartment is on an upper floor.* See Picture 2.

well, *adj.* not sick. *Take these pills and you'll get well soon.*

while, *n.* a time: *We waited a long while. The mailman came a little while ago.*

Idioms

You won't feel a thing. = You won't feel anything.
Open wide. = Open your mouth.
at all = in any way; at any time
next door = in the next house or apartment

Word Study

every

every (four) hours = now, then again after (four) hours, then again after (four) hours

all

all (day/night/weekend/year) = during all of the (day/night/weekend/year)
all these books = all of these books

fill

We **filled** the hole with dirt. (= put something in to the top)
The dentist **filled** the cavity. (= close a cavity by putting something in)
Please **fill** this prescription. (= give the ordered medicine)

compounds with *ache*

Some compounds with *ache* are one word, others are two words.

backache   **stomach ache**
earache
headache
toothache

***get* + adjective**

to get better = to be not so sick; to get well
to get well = to stop being sick

Principal Parts of Verbs

base form	present participle	past tense	past participle
ache	ach ing	ached	ached
drill	drill ing	drilled	drilled
fill	fill ing	filled	filled
hope	hop ing	hoped	hoped
re turn	re turn ing	re turned	re turned

Pronunciation   Sentences with /s/ consonant clusters; final intonation contrasts

A Is this Dr. **Spencer?**

B Yes, it is. What can I do for you?

A This is **Stanley Swing.** Can you help me? My **stomach** aches, my **skin** is red, and I'm **sneezing.**

B When did you get sick?

A At two this morning. I'm **still** sick.

B Did you eat a lot last night?

A No, not much. A **small steak,** some **stuffed** shrimp, some **smooth squash,** a **spring** chicken, and a **slice** of **Steve's sweet strawberry** pie.

Vocabulary Exercise

Choose the correct word.

aches	1. Karen wants to be a dentist, so she's going to _____ school.
clinic	2. Madeleine got _____ soon after the operation.
dental	3. Alex used a _____ to make a hole in the floor.
drill	4. The movie won't start for a _____.
hope	5. The doctor isn't here, but she'll probably _____ soon.
prescription	6. Too much sun can make your _____ red and sore.
return	7. I _____ I get a good grade in English.
skin	8. How many doctors work at that _____?
well	9. My shoulder hurts and my back _____.
while	10. The doctor gave me a _____ for my cough.

GRAMMAR

1. Impersonal *you*

You can mean "everyone" or "people."

You need money to buy a new car. = Everyone needs money to buy a new car.

Do they teach **you** to speak English here? = Do they teach people to speak English here?

2. *-ing* verbal phrases as adjectives

An *-ing* verbal adjective + an object comes after a noun.

The man is wearing a brown hat. He works at the bank.
The man **wearing a brown hat** works at the bank.

The woman is answering the phone. She's the receptionist.
The woman **answering the phone** is the receptionist.

An *-ing* verbal adjective + a prepositional phrase comes after a noun.

The man is driving to the gas station. He has a flat tire.
The man **driving to the gas station** has a flat tire.

The woman is talking to the doctor. She's sick.
The woman **talking to the doctor** is sick.

3. Infinitives after adjectives

I'm **glad to meet** you. = I'm glad I met you.
We're **sorry to hear** that. = We're sorry we heard that.
I'll be **happy to help** you. = I'll be happy I can help you.
They were **sad to leave.** = They were sad that they were leaving.

Exercises

12A: **Impersonal *you*.** Ask and answer. Use Cue Book Chart 5.

orange juice
  STUDENT A Can you get <u>orange juice</u> here?
  STUDENT B No, but you can get <u>tomato juice</u>.

1. pea soup
2. roast chicken
3. baked fish
4. carrots
5. chicken salad

6. lemon pie
7. veal sausage
8. pork chops
9. orange cake
10. a ham sandwich

12B: ***-ing* verbals as adjectives.** Ask and answer. Use Cue Book Chart 4.

was bored/customers/to the singing waiters

    STUDENT A Who <u>was bored</u>?

    STUDENT B The <u>customers</u> <u>listening</u> <u>to the singing waiters</u> <u>were</u> <u>bored</u>.

1. burned the meat/man/in the oven
2. sliced the tomatoes/woman/at the soup
3. was angry/customers/at the receptionist
4. tore the menus/boy/on the desk
5. was very noisy/children/through the restaurant

12C: ***-ing* verbals as adjectives.** Ask and answer. Use Cue Book Chart 2.

boy/your brother/**1**/the sandwich

    STUDENT A Which <u>boy</u> <u>is</u> <u>your brother</u>?

    STUDENT B The <u>one</u> <u>eating</u> <u>the sandwich</u>.

1. woman/the nurse/**2**/coffee
2. girl/your sister/**3**/the tickets
3. man/your father/**4**/the shirts
4. children/your cousins/**5**/the boat
5. woman/the teacher/**6**/the picture
6. man/your uncle/**7**/the newspaper
7. man/a policeman/**8**/the motorcycle
8. woman/the receptionist/**9**/the letter
9. man/the doctor/**10**/the car
10. boy/your son/**1**/the lamb chop

12D: **Infinitives after adjectives.** Ask and answer.

meet my aunt/happy

    STUDENT A Did you <u>meet my aunt</u>?

    STUDENT B Yes, I was <u>happy</u> to <u>meet</u> <u>her</u>.

1. hear the bad news/sorry
2. help Mrs. Taylor/glad
3. sell your house/sorry
4. see Mr. Parker/surprised
5. find your watch/happy

12E: ***It* as subject.** Make a new sentence.

Breaking a bone is awful.

<u>It's awful to break a bone</u>.

1. Getting sick is terrible.
2. Being in the hospital is sad.
3. Buying prescriptions is expensive.
4. Speaking English is easy.
5. Flying a plane is exciting.
6. Going to parties is fun.
7. Having an operation is terrible.
8. Seeing you is wonderful.
9. Watching TV is boring.
10. Finding the clinic is easy.

12F: **Parts of the body.** Ask and answer. Use Cue Book Chart 6.

Bob/clinic/**1**/ache

STUDENT A Did <u>Bob</u> go to the <u>clinic</u>?

STUDENT B Yes, <u>his</u> <u>head</u> <u>aches</u>.

1. Mr. Parker/clinic/**3**/is sore
2. Oscar/clinic/**4**/hurts
3. Joan/clinic/**6**/aches
4. Maria/doctor/**8**/hurts
5. Luisa/hospital/**12**/aches

6. Larry/doctor/**13**/hurts
7. Peter/hospital/**14**/is sore
8. Miss Butler/doctor/**15**/is sore
9. Carlos/dentist/**26**/aches
10. Mrs. Lane/doctor/**27**/aches

12G: **Parts of the body.** Ask and answer. Use Cue Book Chart 6.

1/feel hot/the flu

STUDENT A Does your <u>head</u> <u>feel hot</u>?

STUDENT B Yes, I have <u>the flu</u>.

1. **3**/hurt/a cold
2. **5**/hurt/a sore thumb
3. **10**/hurt/a sore toe
4. **12**/ache/the flu
5. **16**/hurt/a broken bone

6. **18**/feel sore/a toothache
7. **21**/feel sore/a cold
8. **24**/feel dry/a sore throat
9. **26**/ache/a cavity
10. **1**/hurt/a headache

COMMUNICATION PRACTICE

Guided Conversation

DOCTOR What's the matter, <u>Tom</u>?

PATIENT I feel awful. My <u>throat</u> hurts, and I have
a terrible <u>headache</u>.

DOCTOR That's too bad. When did you get sick?

PATIENT Yesterday. I was sick all night.

DOCTOR Here's a prescription. Go to bed and
take <u>two</u> pills every <u>four</u> hours.

PATIENT Thank you, Doctor. I feel better already.

LOOK AT CUE BOOK CHART 6

Activities

A. Ask somebody

Did a doctor ever give you a prescription?
What was it for? Did it make you better?

Maybe you can use . . .

cold	headache
flu	toothache
broken bone	backache
sore throat	stomach ache

B. Talk with somebody.

1. You're sick and you want to go home. Ask a student to take the part of your teacher. Tell him or her about it. The teacher will ask, "Where does it hurt? How are you going to get home?"

2. Joe hurt his knee when he was playing baseball, and now he needs an operation. He's talking to Dr. Sharp and asking a lot of questions. He wants to know, "Will it hurt? How long will I be in the hospital? Can I have visitors? Will I have to wear a cast? When will I be able to walk again? Will I be able to play baseball again?" You and another student take the parts of Joe and Dr. Sharp and perform this conversation.

C. What do you think?

Which are better—old doctors or young ones?
Why do you think so?

Maybe you can use . . .

nicer	more careful
calmer	more friendly
lazier	more helpful
work harder	more forgetful

Self Test

Change the sentence.

I was glad that I met your cousin.
I was glad to meet your cousin.

1. We were surprised when we found you here.
2. She was happy she could help us.
3. They were surprised that they won the game.
4. I was sad when I heard about your broken leg.
5. He was sorry that he was late.

Make one sentence.

The woman is standing at the bus stop. She works at the clinic.
The woman standing at the bus stop works at the clinic.

6. The man is using the drill. He's the dentist.
7. The woman is filling the prescription. She's my aunt.
8. The boy is waiting in the office. He has a toothache.
9. The girl is talking to the receptionist. She wants an appointment.
10. The man is reading the newspaper. He lives next door to us.

LESSON 13

Good Luck*/Bad Luck

***luck** being or not being lucky

READING

Many people believe* that doing certain* things can bring you bad luck or good luck. Do you think this is true? Some people believe these things. Do you agree?

Sneezing is dangerous, because when you sneeze, your soul* can fly out of your body. When somebody sneezes, always say, "God* bless* you." Then the person won't die*.

Always get out of bed on the right side and step on your right foot first, or you'll be unlucky all day. Did you forget and get out of bed on the left side? Back up to the bed, lie down*, and get up again on the right side.

Breaking a mirror can bring you seven years of bad luck, or somebody in your family will die. When you break a mirror, take it outside and bury* it. Then bad things won't happen.

Spilling salt can also bring bad luck. When you spill salt, throw some of it over your left shoulder. That will send the bad luck away from you.

Never walk under a ladder. That brings very bad luck. When you have to walk under a ladder, cross* your fingers.

Black cats are unlucky. When a black cat walks in front of you, go home and start your trip again.

Opening an umbrella in the house is also unlucky. People say, "It makes the sun angry."

What can you do to have good luck? Some people carry a clover* with four leaves. Other people carry a rabbit's foot. Some people say, "Hang a horseshoe* over your door."

A lot of people believe these things can bring bad luck or good luck. Do you?

*to **believe** See New Words.
*certain** See New Words.

*soul(s)** part of a person, not the body
*God** the maker of the world
*to **bless** to help; to give good things to
*to **die** to stop living
*to **lie down** See New Words.

*to **bury** to put under the ground

*to **cross** to put (one thing) across (another). See Idioms.

*clover**
*horseshoe(s)**

Questions

1. Why do some people think sneezing is dangerous?
2. What do some people believe will happen when you break a mirror?
3. Do you carry something to bring you good luck? What is it?

VOCABULARY

New Words

al′pha bet′i cal, *adj.* in order, like the letters of the alphabet: *He wrote the words in alphabetical order.*

to be lieve′, *v.* To think something is true: *Most people believe the world is round.*

cer′tain, *adj.* some; different; of one kind: *Certain people are never lucky.*

def′i ni′tion(s), *n.* meaning: *What's the definition of lucky?*

to lie′ down′, *v.* to put the body down on a bed, couch, or floor: *The girl lay down and went to sleep.*

or′der, *n.* one thing coming after another in a certain way: *The boxes stood on the shelf in order of size.*

part′(s) of speech′, *n.* the way to use a word in a sentence: *Nouns, verbs, and adjectives are parts of speech.*

pro nun′ci a′tion(s), *n.* way of saying words: *Our teacher's pronunciation is easy to understand.*

Idioms

He **crossed his fingers.**

Principal Parts of Verbs

base form	present participle	past tense	past participle
be lieve	be liev ing	be lieved	be lieved
lie down	ly ing down	lay down	lain down

READING AND WRITING SKILLS

1. Alphabetical order

Words in an English dictionary are always in alphabetical order. Look at New Words. They're in alphabetical order.

When you are putting words in alphabetical order, look at the first letter of each word. When the first letters are the same, look at the second letters. When the first and second letters are the same, look at the third letters.

2. Parts of speech

Dictionaries tell you parts of speech. Look at New Words. The part of speech is between the word and the definition.

Sometimes a word can be more than one part of speech. A dictionary will tell you that. Look at New Words in Lesson 12. *Ache* and *drill* can be nouns or verbs.

3. Pronunciation

Dictionaries tell you the pronunciations of words. How many syllables does a word have? Where is the accent? A dictionary will tell you.

4. Definitions

Dictionaries give definitions of words. Look at New Words. The definition comes after the part of speech. There's a sentence after the definition. It helps tell the meaning of the word.

Sometimes a word has more than one definition. A dictionary will tell you that. Look at New Words in Lesson 12. How many definitions does *return* have?

Exercises

13A: **Alphabetical order.** Write each group of words in alphabetical order.

1. valley, artificial, patient, medicine, boil, shaker, wide, emergency, clinic, garlic
2. travel, hood, sausage, narrow, natural, toothache, highway, sheep, pig, pain
3. broil, flat, recipe, flu, block, form, return, receptionist, battery, bake

13B: **Parts of speech.** Write the parts of speech for these words. Look at New Words in Lesson 9. Remember, some words can be more than one part of speech. (Look at Abbreviations on page 142 and write the whole words.)

1. broil	3. chocolate	5. forgetful	7. instead	9. vanilla
2. chef	4. egg	6. fry	8. sweet	10. vinegar

13C: **Definitions.** Write each sentence again without using the word in dark letters. Look at New Words in Lesson 8.

1. Would you like a **beverage?**
2. These flowers are **artificial.**
3. I won't eat in that restaurant **anymore.**
4. We left the waitress a **tip.**
5. When are you going to **serve** the entree?

13D: **Definitions.** Write each sentence again without using the word or words in dark letters. Look at New Words in Lesson 11.

1. Are you calm in **a time when you have to do something right now?**
2. **The inside of** my **neck** is sore.
3. What **other things** do you want to know?
4. Does your cousin know the **person seeing the doctor?**
5. I have a terrible **hurting** in my back.

COMMUNICATION PRACTICE

Writing Activities

A. Some people think the number 13 is unlucky. Other people have "lucky numbers." Do you think numbers can be lucky or unlucky? Do you have a lucky or unlucky number? What is it? Why do you think that number is lucky or unlucky? Write a paragraph to answer these questions.

B. Some people think these things are unlucky: to put a hat on a bed, to sing before breakfast, to carry a cat into the house, to start a trip on Friday, to wear green clothes on stage, to point at the moon. Do you think any of these things is unlucky? Do you think anything else is unlucky? What do your friends think is unlucky? Write a paragraph about unlucky things.

Unit Self Test

Complete the sentence with the correct reflexive pronoun.

1. I baked it _____.
2. They washed _____ in the river.
3. She grew the tomatoes _____.
4. He cooked _____ a big breakfast.
5. Did you and your husband buy _____ a new car?

Make one sentence.

6. The woman is talking on the phone. She's the receptionist.
7. The man is sitting in the office. He hurt his leg.
8. The girls are standing in line. They want to buy tickets.
9. The boy is sitting in the dentist's chair. He has a toothache.
10. The people are eating in the restaurant. They're happy.

LESSON 14

Stop, thief!

CONVERSATIONS

1.

MRS. VANDERGILT Young man, I've been here for ten minutes. Would you please wait on me?

YOUNG MAN I'm sorry, ma'am. I can't.

MRS. VANDERGILT What do you mean—you can't? Of course you can. Is this camera on sale?

YOUNG MAN Ma'am, you'll have to wait for . . .

MRS. VANDERGILT I beg your pardon. *I'm* Abigail Vandergilt, and I do *not* like to wait! Now please show me your least expensive camera.

YOUNG MAN But I really can't help you. I don't . . .

MRS. VANDERGILT How insulting! I want to see the manager!

2.

MANAGER I understand you're too busy to help Mrs. Vandergilt, our richest . . . I mean, our *best* customer.

YOUNG MAN No, sir. I'm not too busy. I just don't . . .

MANAGER You just don't work in this shop anymore. You're fired!

3.

MANAGER There. I've taken care of everything.

MRS. VANDERGILT Thank you. No one has ever treated me as badly as that impolite young man.

MANAGER Hey! Look at him now! He's stealing the cash register! Stop, thief!

YOUNG MAN Sir, I'm not stealing it!

MANAGER Well, what *are* you doing then?

YOUNG MAN I've tried to tell you. I'm not a clerk here. I repair cash registers. This one won't open, and all of the store's money is inside.

MANAGER The money?!?! Here, let me help you! Where's your hammer? Mrs. Vandergilt, would you please get out of the way!!!!

Questions

1. Why was Mrs. Vandergilt angry?
2. Why didn't the young man wait on her?
3. Has a clerk or waiter ever been impolite to you? What happened?

VOCABULARY

New Words

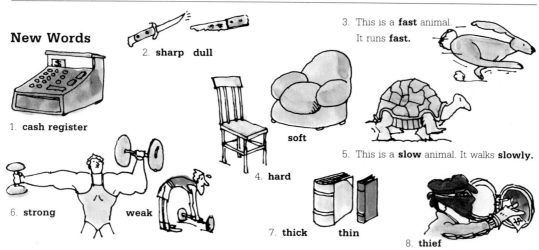

1. cash register
2. sharp   dull
3. This is a **fast** animal. It runs **fast**.
4. hard
5. This is a **slow** animal. It walks **slowly**.
6. strong   weak
7. thick   thin
   soft
8. thief

best, *adv.* See Grammar.

bet'ter, *adv.* See Grammar.

cash' reg'is ter(s), *n.* The clerk put the money in the cash register. See Picture 1.

com'fort a ble, *adj.* feeling good; making things easier: *A soft, warm bed is comfortable.*

com'pli cat ed, *adj.* hard to understand: *Computers are complicated.*

dull, *adj.* not able to cut things: *I can't use these dull scissors.* See Picture 2.

dur'a ble, *adj.* able to last a long time: *I need a durable jacket for winter.*

fast, *adj.* *We took the fast train to Rome. adv. Airplanes go fast.* See Picture 3.

hard, *adj.* like glass or rock: *Don't sit on that hard bench.* See Picture 4.

im po lite', *adj.* not polite: *The customer didn't leave a tip for the impolite waiter.*

in'ex pen'sive, *adj.* not expensive: *She didn't have much money, so she bought an inexpensive lunch.*

to in sult', *v.* to hurt with words: *The woman insulted Tom when she laughed at his tie.*

least, *adv.* See Grammar.

less, *adv.* See Grammar.

lit'tle, *adj.* not much: *I was thirsty, so I drank a little water.*

man'a ger(s), *n.* the boss: *The manager was angry because the workers came late.*

pleas'ant, *adj.* good, nice: *The clerks in that store are always pleasant.*

po lite', *adj.* acting in a good way; nice: *The polite girl gave the old man her chair.*

sale(s), *n.* selling: *They were happy about the sale of their house.*

sharp, *adj.* able to cut things easily; not dull: *This knife is easy to use because it's very sharp.* See Picture 2.

slow, *adj. We sang a slow song.* See Picture 5.

soft, *adj.* not hard: *The baby has very soft skin.* See Picture 4.

to steal, *v.* to take something not belonging to you: *Somebody stole all my money!*

strong, *adj. We need a strong rope to tie these boxes.* See Picture 6.

stur′dy, *adj.* strong; durable: *The fat woman needed a sturdy chair.*

to take′ care′ of, *v.* to watch over; to do things for; to do something about: *I take care of my little sister when my parents aren't home. The secretary takes care of answering the mail.*

thick, *adj. He ate a thick piece of bread.* See Picture 7.

thief (thieves), *n. A thief stole the manager's car!* See Picture 8.

thin, *adj.* not thick: *It was hot, so she wore a thin dress.* See Picture 7.

to treat, *v.* to act toward: *The children treated the kitten with love.*

weak, *adj.* not strong: *He's weak because he has the flu.* See Picture 6.

worse, *adv.* See Grammar.

worst, *adv.* See Grammar.

Idioms

to be fired = to lose your job; to have your job taken away from you

I beg your pardon. = Excuse me.

sale

This car is **for sale.** (= ready to sell)

Cameras are **on sale** this week. (= for sale at a lower price than usually)

They're **having a sale on** shirts. (= selling at a lower price than usually)

get out of

Get out of the way. (= move to another place)

What time do you **get out of** school? (= leave)

What did you **get out of** that class? (= learn from)

Word Study

Adverbs ending in -*ly*

This is a slow bus. It travels very **slowly.**

That nurse is very polite. She spoke **politely.**

Marcia has a pleasant voice. She sings **pleasantly.**

The baby is happy. He's playing **happily.**

Principal Parts of Verbs

base form	present participle	past tense	past participle
in sult	in sult ing	in sult ed	in sult ed
steal	steal ing	stole	stol en
take care of	tak ing care of	took care of	tak en care of
treat	treat ing	treat ed	treat ed

Pronunciation   Sentences with Key Words TABLE /t/, DESK /d/, THIN /θ/, THAT /ð/; intonation in direct address and comparisons

Tina, this is *the fourth time.*

Doctor, do you *take patients* on *Tuesdays?*

Sue, *the Tracys want three things.*

Theda, do you like *thin* people?

Did anybody hear *Thursday's* program, *Ted?*

Please *write these letters, Edward.*

Mom *sounds* more *tired than Dad.*

Tim rode faster than Ted.

The theater is *wider than the hospital.*

Tom traveled farther than Theo.

Thad ordered more *than Thelma.*

That thief is worse *than the other* one.

Vocabulary Exercise

Choose the correct word.

comfortable

complicated

dull

fast

impolite

inexpensive

stole

strong

thick

treats

1. Joe bought a car with a big engine because he likes to go _____.
2. The woman called the manager because the clerk was _____ to her.
3. I can't do my math because it's too _____.
4. Stop that man! He _____ all my money!
5. She didn't sit on the hard chair because it wasn't _____.
6. That doctor always _____ her patients politely.
7. He couldn't cut the meat because the knife was too _____.
8. The old house had _____ stone walls.
9. We didn't have much money, so we stayed at an _____ motel.
10. I can't move the bookcase because I'm not very _____.

GRAMMAR

1. *a few/fewer/the fewest, a little/less/the least*

Use *a few*, *fewer*, and *the fewest* with count nouns.
Use *a little*, *less*, and *the least* with mass nouns.

Tom ate six strawberries. He ate **a few** strawberries.
Mary ate four strawberries. She ate **fewer** strawberries than Tom.
Joe ate two strawberries. He ate **the fewest** strawberries.

Maria ate four pieces of cheese. She ate **a little** cheese.
Rudy ate three pieces of cheese. He ate **less** cheese than Maria.
Max ate one piece of cheese. He ate **the least** cheese.

2. *Less* and *the least* in comparative and superlative adjectives

Carlos is always polite.
Sometimes Fred isn't polite. He's **less polite** than Carlos.
Hector is never polite. He's **the least polite** of all the boys.
　　　　　　　　　　He's **the least polite** boy in the class.

3. *too* + adjective + *to*

I can't carry that table because it's too heavy.
That table is **too heavy to** carry.

4. Comparative and superlative adverbs

Birds fly fast.
Planes fly **faster** than birds.
Birds don't fly **as fast as** planes.
Which plane flies **the fastest?**

Bob acted impolitely.
Laura acted **more impolitely** than Bob.
Susan acted **as impolitely as** Laura.
Rita acted **the most impolitely.**

Gene works carefully.
Robert works **less carefully** than Gene.
George doesn't work **as carefully as** Robert.
George works **the least carefully.**

Mary sings **well.**
Lucy sings **better** than Mary.
They don't sing **as well as** Joan.
Joan sings **the best** of anyone in class.

The soccer team played **badly.**
The tennis team played **worse.**
They didn't play **as badly as** the golf team.
The golf team played **the worst.**

Exercises

14A: ***a few/a little.*** Ask and answer.

apples   STUDENT A   How <u>many</u> <u>apples</u> did you eat?
            STUDENT B   I ate <u>a few</u> <u>apples</u>.

cheese   STUDENT C   How <u>much</u> <u>cheese</u> did you eat?
            STUDENT D   I ate <u>a little</u> <u>cheese</u>.

1. bread	3. raspberries	5. beef	7. strawberries	9. garlic
2. carrots	4. beets	6. cabbage	8. grapes	10. cereal

14B: ***fewer/the fewest/less/the least.*** Complete the sentences.

Bill has a bag of fruit. Betsy has six bags of fruit. Tom has two bags of fruit.
1. Tom has _____ fruit than Betsy.
2. Tom has _____ fruit than Bill.
3. Bill has _____ fruit than Betsy.
4. Bill has _____ fruit.
5. Betsy has _____ fruit.

Alice has seven books. Elaine has ten books. Eric has four books.
6. Alice has _____ books than Elaine.
7. Alice has _____ books than Eric.
8. Eric has _____ books than Elaine.
9. Elaine has _____ books.
10. Eric has _____ books.

14C: **Comparative adjectives.** Complete the sentence. Use *less* or *more*.

(intelligent)   Mary passed all of her courses. Kim failed all of hers.
                 Kim is <u>less intelligent</u> than Mary.

1. (comfortable)   The blue chair is hard. The red chair is soft.
                   The red chair is _____ than the blue one.
2. (complicated)   Computers are hard to use. Cash registers are easy to use.
                   Cash registers are _____ than computers.
3. (expensive)   The radio is expensive. The cassette player is inexpensive.
                   The cassette player is _____ than the radio.
4. (pleasant)   The manager was insulting. The clerk was polite.
                   The clerk was _____ than the manager.
5. (durable)   The record player broke after a month. The TV lasted a year.
                   The TV was _____ than the record player.

14D: **Comparative adverbs.** Ask and answer.

sing/beautiful

   STUDENT A Do you <u>sing</u> as <u>beautifully</u> as your cousin?
   STUDENT B Oh, I <u>sing</u> more <u>beautifully</u> than my cousin!

1. write/clever   4. drive/dangerous
2. learn/easy   5. move/slow
3. shout/angry

14E: **Comparative and superlative adverbs.** Complete the sentences.

1. A bus goes fast. A train goes _____ than a bus. A plane goes _____.
2. Andy gets up early. Carl gets up _____ than Andy. Mike gets up _____.
3. Carol writes well. Charley writes _____ than Carol. Virginia writes _____.
4. The boys talked loud. The girls talked _____ than the boys. The teacher talked _____.
5. Martha played badly. Tom played _____ than Martha. Rita played _____.

14F: *too + adjective + to.* Make a new sentence.

That chair is hard. Don't sit on it.
<u>That chair is too hard to sit on.</u>

1. That bench is weak. Don't sit on it.   4. This paper is too thin. Don't write on it.
2. This sandwich is too thick. I can't bite it.   5. The ice is soft. Don't skate on it.
3. That horse is too fast. Don't ride it.

COMMUNICATION PRACTICE

Guided Conversation

CUSTOMER I beg your pardon. Could you help me?
    CLERK Why, certainly. What can I do for you?
CUSTOMER I'd like to see a <u>calculator</u>.
    CLERK All right. Here's a nice one. It's our least expensive <u>calculator</u>.
CUSTOMER It doesn't look very <u>durable</u>.
    CLERK Perhaps you'd like this one. It costs more, but it works a lot better.
CUSTOMER That looks fine. I'll take it.

DURABLE

STURDY

SHARP

Activities

A. Ask somebody.

Have you ever bought anything on sale? What?
Were you happy because you bought it? Why?

Maybe you can use . . .

durable	broke very soon
sturdy	lasted a long time
inexpensive	didn't fit
beautiful	
comfortable	

B. Talk with somebody.

1. Some people can sell anything to anybody. Can you? Try to sell your desk or chair to the
   student sitting next to you. That student doesn't want to buy it, so you'll have to say
   wonderful things about it. Use adjectives like *beautiful, comfortable, sturdy, durable,* and
   inexpensive. Look at the Guided Conversation for more ideas.

2. Mrs. Holiday is angry. She just got back from a vacation hotel near a lake, and she had
   an awful time. Her room was very small, and it was too noisy to sleep in. The waiters in
   the restaurant were slow and impolite, and the food was too terrible to eat. The tennis
   courts were old and dirty, the lake was too dangerous to swim in, and the golf teacher
   was insulting. Now Mrs. Holiday is talking to Mr. Booker, the travel agent. He
   recommended the hotel and made all of the reservations. You and another student
   perform the conversation between Mrs. Holiday and Mr. Booker. What does she tell him?
   What does he say to her? Will she ever ask him for reservations again?

C. What do you think?

Is it always better to buy things on sale? Why?

Self Test

Complete the sentence. Use *a little* or *a few*.

1. Tom wasn't hungry, so he ate only _____ soup.
2. Marcia bought _____ raspberries.
3. She's going to cook _____ beets for dinner.
4. I'd like _____ ice cream, please.
5. Do you want _____ butter for your roll?

Complete the sentence. Use a comparative or superlative adverb.

6. (fast)   He runs _____ than anybody else on the team.
7. (badly)   I play chess _____ than Carl does.
8. (loud)   The girl in the red shirt talked _____ of all the students.
9. (well)   Carol sings _____ than Lorna.
10. (carefully) Which student in the class works _____?

LESSON 15

Will that be cash or charge?

CONVERSATIONS

1.

CUSTOMER Where are the shirts that are on sale?

MISS TELLER They're in aisle three, near the elevator.

CUSTOMER Thank you.

2.

CUSTOMER Excuse me, ma'am. Could you help me?

MRS. SELLERS Of course.

CUSTOMER I'm looking for the shirts that are on sale. The ones that were in the ad in the paper had long sleeves, but these all have short sleeves.

MRS. SELLERS There are plenty of long-sleeved shirts on the counter behind you.

CUSTOMER Are they washable?

MRS. SELLERS Yes. The washing instructions are on the tags.

3.

MR. WALKER Can I help you?

CUSTOMER I'm looking for the clerk who was waiting on me. I've decided to buy these two shirts.

MR. WALKER I'll take care of it. Will that be cash or charge?

CUSTOMER Cash. Do you charge for gift wrapping?

MR. WALKER No, gift wrapping is free.

CUSTOMER Good. They're a birthday present for my brother.

MR. WALKER All right. Just wait a few minutes and I'll wrap them and bring you your change.

CUSTOMER Thank you.

Questions

1. What did the customer want to buy? Why?
2. How did the customer pay for the shirts?
3. Do you usually charge things or pay cash? Why?

VOCABULARY

New Words

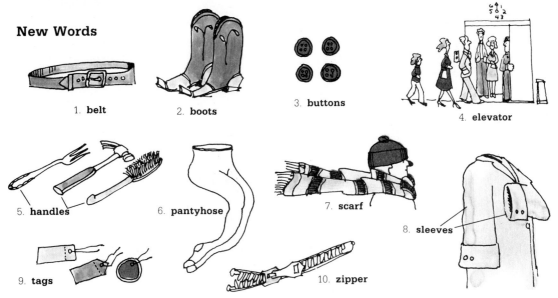

1. **belt**
2. **boots**
3. **buttons**
4. **elevator**
5. **handles**
6. **pantyhose**
7. **scarf**
8. **sleeves**
9. **tags**
10. **zipper**

to ad'ver tise, *v.* to tell about in an ad:
Stores often advertise on the radio.

aisle(s), *n.* a long, empty place between
lines of seats in a theater, church, or
school, or between counters in a store:
*At the movies, I always sit near the
aisle.*

belt(s), *n. Her dress has a wide, blue belt.*
See Picture 1.

bill(s), *n.* a paper with the cost of work
done or things bought: *My dentist sent
me a bill for filling my cavity.*

boot(s), *n. The children wore boots to
play in the snow.* See Picture 2.

but'ton(s), *n.* 1. *I lost one of the buttons
from my shirt.* See Picture 3. 2. a thing
to push for something to work: *Push
this button to start the car.*

cash, *n.* money: *How much cash do you
have?*

to cash, *v.* 1. to give money for: *This store
doesn't cash checks.* 2. to get money
for: *You can cash your check at the
bank.*

change, *n.* money given back to you

when you pay more than the price of
something: *I'll give the waitress a tip
when she brings my change.*

to charge, *v.* 1. to ask as a price: *How much
does that store charge for lamb chops?*
2. to agree to pay for something later:
*She didn't have any cash with her, so
she charged her lunch.*

check(s), *n.* a paper telling a bank to pay
money to the person named: *My
parents pay most of their bills by check.*

cloth'ing, *n.* clothes: *I bought my skirt at
the clothing store.*

el'e va'tor(s), *n.* a moving floor or small
room to carry things or people up and
down in a building: *They took the
elevator upstairs.* See Picture 4.

free, *adj.* not costing anything: *These
tickets were free.*

han'dle(s), *n.* the part of a thing to hold:
The handle of this spoon is broken. See
Picture 5.

in'for ma'tion, *n.* things known; news:
*A dictionary has information about
words.*

in struc'tions, *n.* directions: *He didn't understand the teacher's instructions.*

pan'ty hose, *n. She tore her pantyhose on the corner of her chair.* See Picture 6.

plen'ty, *adj.* enough: *I have plenty of money to buy lunch.*

price(s), *n.* cost: *What's the price of this hat?*

scarf(s), *n. Wrap your scarf around your neck to keep warm.* See Picture 7.

sleeve(s), *n. The sleeves of his new jacket are too long.* See Picture 8.

tag(s), *n.* a piece of paper tied or fastened to something: *Each coat in the store has a tag with its price on it.* See Picture 9.

use'ful, *adj.* helpful; good to use: *My calculator is useful for doing my math.*

wash'a ble, *adj.* able to be washed: *I didn't buy the sweater because it wasn't washable.*

zip'per(s), *n. Do you want a coat with buttons or with a zipper?* See Picture 10.

Idioms

Word Study

Hyphenated adjectives

This shirt has short sleeves. It's a **short-sleeved** shirt.
The rooms in that house have high ceilings. I like **high-ceilinged** rooms.
The toes of her shoes are open. She always wears **open-toed** shoes.
The brush has a long handle. It's a **long-handled** brush.

Principal Parts of Verbs

base form	present participle	past tense	past participle
ad ver tise	ad ver tis ing	ad ver tised	ad ver tised
cash	cash ing	cashed	cashed
charge	charg ing	charged	charged

Pronunciation   Sentences with /l/r/ consonant clusters; intonation in alternatives and contrasts

You can have a **blue blanket** or a **brown** one.
Grace will take a **plane** or a **train.**
Mr. **Fry probably drives** or **flies.**
We didn't **bring plates** or **glasses.**
That's a **credit** card, not a **driver's** license.
Play with the **presents,** not the **prizes.**

Is it easier to **dry fruit** or **flowers?**
Will you **travel** in **Greece** or **Brazil?**
Is the **crowd** in the **classroom** or the **clinic?**
He can't **drink grapefruit** or **grape** juice.
The **driver** was either **Greg** or **Clark.**
Order **fried shrimp** or **broiled** chicken.

Vocabulary Exercise

Choose the correct word.

advertised	1. You don't need any money because the movie is _____.
aisle	2. I was too tired to walk upstairs, so I took the _____.
bill	3. The passengers were standing in the _____ of the bus.
cash	4. The clothing store _____ a sale on winter coats.
check	5. The mechanic sent me a _____ for repairing my car.
elevator	6. You can pay this bill with a _____ or with a credit card.
free	7. She tied her _____ around her neck.
price	8. The _____ of each shirt is on the tag.
scarf	9. I can't wear my jacket because the _____ is broken.
zipper	10. He's going to the bank to _____ a check.

GRAMMAR

Relative clauses with subject pronouns

A relative clause describes the noun before it.
A pronoun begins a relative clause.
The pronoun is *who* for people and *that* for things and animals.

I talked to the dentist. She works in that clinic.
I talked to the dentist **who works in that clinic.**

He bought a computer. It plays music.
He bought a computer **that plays music.**

A doctor was on the plane. He gave the passengers some pills.
The doctor **who was on the plane** gave the passengers some pills.

A dog bit the little boy. The dog didn't hurt him.
The dog **that bit the little boy** didn't hurt him.

A girl is buying some black boots. I don't know her.
I don't know the girl **who's buying the black boots.**

Joe's button fell on the floor. He can't find it.
Joe can't find the button **that fell on the floor.**

Exercises

15A: **Relative clauses with subject pronouns.** Ask and answer.

movies/are funny
> STUDENT A What kind of <u>movies</u> do you like?
> STUDENT B I like <u>movies</u> that <u>are funny</u>.

1. cars/go fast
2. jobs/are easy
3. games/aren't complicated
4. dental drills/don't hurt
5. drinks/are sweet
6. stores/advertise plenty of sales
7. articles/are useful
8. coats/have zippers
9. apartment buildings/have elevators
10. shirts/are washable

15B: **Relative clauses with subject pronouns.** Ask and answer. Use Cue Book Chart 1.

2/the girl/wants a job
> STUDENT A Did <u>you</u> get a letter?
> STUDENT B Yes. It was from <u>the girl</u> <u>who wants a job</u>.

1. **3**/the manager/insulted us
2. **4**/the man/found their dog
3. **5**/the customer/stole the cash register
4. **6**/the clerk/cashed the check
5. **7**/the woman/bought the pantyhose

15C: **Relative clauses with subject pronouns.** Make one sentence. Use *who*.

Some of the girls own motorcycles. They ride them to school.
<u>The girls who own motorcycles ride them to school.</u>

One of the children won the game. He was happy.
<u>The child who won the game was happy.</u>

1. Some of the students spoke English. They answered my questions.
2. One of the clerks sold me a belt. He gave me my change.
3. One of the boys had a sharp knife. He cut himself.
4. One of the women bought some buttons. She's making a blouse.
5. Some of the men were wearing scarfs. They were working outside.

15D: **Relative clauses with subject pronouns.** Make one sentence. Use *that.*

One of the lions was hiding in the field. It ate the lamb.
The lion that was hiding in the field ate the lamb.

Some of the spoons are on the table. They have broken handles.
The spoons that are on the table have broken handles.

1. One of the cash registers doesn't work. It's on the floor.
2. Some of the planes ran into the storm. They arrived late.
3. One of the cars runs well. It's mine.
4. Some of the bills are from the department store. They're in the desk.
5. One of the books is on my desk. It's from the library.

15E: **Relative clauses with subject pronouns.** Choose a good ending for each sentence.

1. Teachers like students
2. Students like teachers
3. Children like parents
4. Parents like children
5. Nobody likes people

a. who don't cry.
b. who never shout at them.
c. who are always angry.
d. who do their homework.
e. who give good grades.

15F: **Vocabulary.** Say the opposite.

1. She always uses knives that are <u>dull</u>.
2. He usually uses ropes that are <u>weak</u>.
3. That restaurant has waiters who are <u>slow</u>.
4. We never drive on roads that are <u>narrow</u>.
5. I like to sit on chairs that are <u>hard</u>.

15G: **Vocabulary.** Say the opposite.

least pleasant   most interesting   most polite   most popular   most unlucky

1. The clerk who was the <u>most impolite</u> doesn't work here anymore.
2. The boys who were the <u>luckiest</u> were on my team.
3. The receptionist who was the <u>nicest</u> answered the phone.
4. They heard the speaker who was the <u>most boring</u>.
5. I always like the singers who are the <u>most unpopular</u>.

15H: **Relative clauses with subject pronouns.** Make one sentence. Use *who* or *that*.

They met a woman. She knows their parents.
They met a woman who knows their parents.

I read about a computer. It can play chess.
I read about a computer that can play chess.

1. He talked to a girl. She wants to be a restaurant manager.
2. I waited on a customer. He used a credit card.
3. She couldn't find the boots. They were on sale.
4. Are you going to pay the bills? They're on the desk.
5. She wants to buy a jacket. It has buttons.

15I: **Relative clauses with subject pronouns.** Make one sentence. Use *who* or *that*.

The store advertised shirts on sale. It's closed today.
The store that advertised shirts on sale is closed today.

The man repaired the cash register. He sent me a bill.
The man who repaired the cash register sent me a bill.

1. The clerk works in the shoe department. She's very pleasant.
2. The shirts have long sleeves. They're more expensive.
3. The woman bought some pantyhose. She paid by check.
4. The man cashed my check. He didn't give me my change.
5. The book has information about advertising. It's on the table.

COMMUNICATION PRACTICE

Guided Conversation

CLERK Can I help you?
CUSTOMER Yes. I'd like to see the <u>boots</u> that are on sale.
CLERK Here they are. They're very nice. They're <u>sturdy</u> and they're <u>inexpensive</u>.
CUSTOMER Fine. I'll take these.
CLERK All right. Will that be cash or charge?
CUSTOMER <u>Charge</u>.

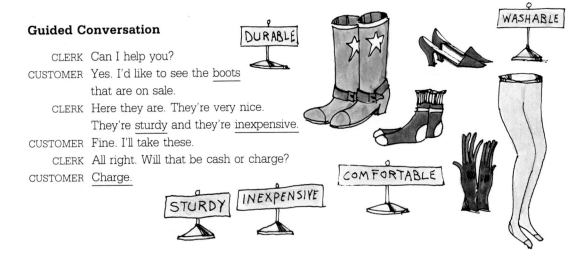

Activities

A. Ask somebody.

Do you ever charge things in department stores?

Do you ever charge meals in restaurants?

Do you pay your bills with cash or by check?

B. Talk with somebody.

1. You want to eat dinner in a restaurant, but you don't have any cash. Call the restaurant and talk to the manager. Do they take credit cards? Can you pay by check? Ask another student to take the part of the restaurant manager and perform the conversation with you.

2. A parent wants to buy a winter jacket for a child. The parent wants a jacket that is warm, sturdy, durable, and inexpensive. The child wants a blue jacket with a zipper instead of buttons. The clerk who waits on them tries to be very polite and shows them a lot of jackets. The customers don't like any of them—one is too thin, one is too short, one is brown, one has buttons, and they're all too expensive. At last the parent decides to go to another store. The clerk still tries to be pleasant, but is really happy because they're leaving. You and another student take the parts of the parent and the clerk and perform this conversation. (The clerk should look at the Guided Conversation for ideas.)

C. What do you think?

Is it better to charge things or to pay cash? Why?

Maybe you can use . . .

easy	carry a lot of cash
useful	get big bills
expensive	

Self Test

Make one sentence. Use *who* or *that*.

1. The teacher explained the exercise to the students. They stayed after class.
2. She bought some pantyhose. They were on sale.
3. Did you pick up the check? It was on the hall table.
4. We talked to the travel agent. He made the reservations.
5. He likes the short-sleeved shirt. It's in the window.

LESSON 16

I want my money back!

CONVERSATIONS

1.

MANAGER   We have a part-time job in our complaint department. You'll answer customers' complaints, exchange things that are the wrong size or color, and give people their money back if something is broken or doesn't work.

MISS HANDEL   That sounds interesting.

2.

MRS. SMALL   I want to return this sweater. I washed it, and now it's too tight.

MISS HANDEL   Oh, ma'am, wool sweaters always shrink if you wash them.

MRS. SMALL   But the tag says "washable." Look.

MISS HANDEL   You're right. Would you like to exchange this for another sweater, or do you want your money back?

MRS. SMALL   I'd like another sweater.

MISS HANDEL   Fine. Why don't you look at the Orlon sweaters? Orlon never shrinks.

MRS. SMALL   Thank you. I'll do that.

3.

MR. FARAD   This toy car doesn't work!

MISS HANDEL   What seems to be the matter with it?

MR. FARAD   Look. The instructions say, "Push the button, and the engine will run." Well, I pushed it, but nothing happened.

MISS HANDEL   I see the problem. This is an electric car. The instructions also say, "Use two flashlight batteries." If you put two batteries in it, it'll work.

MR. FARAD   Oh, I see. Thank you. I'm sorry I bothered you.

MISS HANDEL   That's all right, sir.

Questions

1. What was Mrs. Small's complaint?
2. What did Mr. Farad complain about?
3. Have you ever had a part-time job? What was it?

VOCABULARY

New Words

1. **cotton**

2. These radios are **electric.**

3. **screen**

4. Her sweater is **loose.** It **stretched.**   5. His sweater is **tight.** It **shrank.**

6. **thread**

to both′er, *v.* to worry, to make angry, to give a problem to: *Hot weather bothers me.*

cloth, *n.* material made of threads fastened together: *Clothing, curtains, sheets, and towels are made of cloth.*

to com plain′, *v.* to tell about something that is wrong: *We complained because the room was too cold.*

com plaint′(s), *n.* a complaining: *She had a lot of complaints about the hotel's food.*

cot′ton, *n.* soft, light thread or cloth made from part of a plant: *Blue jeans are made of cotton.* See Picture 1. *adj.* made of cotton: *a cotton shirt; cotton sheets.*

e lec′tric, *adj.* *After the storm, the electric lights didn't work.* See Picture 2.

to ex change′, *v.* to give for another thing: *I exchanged the blue shirt for a green one.*

full′-time′, *adj.* for all of the time: *He has a full-time job as a mechanic.*

fur, *n.* the soft hair of many animals: *Bears have thick fur. adj.* made of fur: *a fur coat; fur boots.*

if, *conj.* See Grammar.

leath′er, *n.* the skin of some animals: *Shoes are often made of leather. adj.* made of leather: *a leather belt; leather gloves.*

loose, *adj.* not tight: *The jacket was too loose, so he got a smaller size.* See Picture 4.

made′ of, *adj.* built, made, or put together from (a material): *Desks and chairs are usually made of wood.*

ma ter′i al(s), *n.* the thing or things that something is made of: *Cloth, thread, buttons, and zippers are dress materials.*

ny′lon, *n.* a strong, durable, synthetic material that can stretch without breaking: *A rope made of nylon is very strong. adj.* made of nylon: *a nylon blouse; nylon pantyhose.*

Or′lon, *n.* a light, strong, synthetic material that sun and water can't hurt: *Raincoats made of Orlon are warm and comfortable. adj.* made of Orlon: *an Orlon sweater; Orlon socks.*

part′-time′, *adj.* for part of the time: *I have a part-time job after school.*

plas′tic, *n.* a very strong, sturdy, synthetic material that can be hard like glass or soft like cloth: *These dishes are made of plastic. adj.* made of plastic: *a plastic bottle; a plastic tablecloth.*

prob′lem(s), *n.* something that is difficult; something to figure out: *The manager of a large company has to take care of a lot of problems. He did all of his math problems.*

screen(s), *n. That TV has a very small screen.* See Picture 3.

to shrink, *v.* 1. to make smaller: *He shrank his sweater when he washed it.* 2. to get smaller: *Wool shrinks in hot water.* See Picture 5.

to stretch, *v.* 1. to make bigger: *Her sweater was too tight, so she stretched it.* 2. to get bigger: *The rope stretched.* See Picture 4.

syn thet′ic, *adj.* artificial: *Nylon and Orlon are synthetic materials.*

tel′e vi′sion, *n.* TV: *Let's watch television.*

thread, *n. I need some thread to fix the hole in my shirt.* See Picture 6.

tight, *adj.* fitting closely: *He needs a bigger shirt because this one's too tight.* See Picture 5.

toy(s), *n.* something for a child to play with: *Balls and electric trains are toys.*

wood, *n.* the hard part of a tree: *Houses, boats, and chairs are often made of wood.*

wood′en, *adj.* made of wood: *a wooden chair; wooden steps.*

wool, *n.* the soft hair of a sheep: *The farmer sold the wool from his sheep. adj.* made of wool: *a wool coat; wool pants.*

Idiom

INFORMAL **What's the matter?**

FORMAL **What seems to be the matter?**

Word Study

work/play/run

In English, many things "work."

He went too fast because his speedometer **didn't work.**

The cash register **wasn't working,** so she tried to fix it.

Does this radio **work?**

That old clock usually **works** well.

Nothing on this car **works** correctly!

Things that make noise can also "play."

A tape recorder **won't play** when the batteries are dead.

Their radio **played** all night.

Clocks and things with engines can also "run."

Is your watch **running?**

Her new car **runs** well.

The powerboat **ran** very noisily.

full-time/part-time

A **full-time** job is usually for 7 or 8 hours a day and for 5 or 6 days a week.

A **part-time** job is for only a few hours a day or for only a few days a week.

Principal Parts of Verbs

base form	present participle	past tense	past participle
both er	both er ing	both ered	both ered
com plain	com plain ing	com plained	com plained
ex change	ex chang ing	ex changed	ex changed
shrink	shrink ing	shrank	shrunk
stretch	stretch ing	stretched	stretched

Pronunciation   Sentences with final nasal consonant clusters; non-final intonation in clauses with _if_

If you **want** natural material, buy **cotton.**

What can I do if the cotton **shrinks?**

It **won't shrink** if you wash it carefully.

If he **owns** that farm, it **belongs** to him.

He works twelve **months** a year on it.

If the work is hard, he **finds assistants.**

If you have **problems,** talk to Mrs. **Trant.**

She's in the **complaint department.**

If she **can't** help you, nobody can.

What **happened** to those broken **lamps?**

I **exchanged** them for new **ones.**

If you **exchanged** the **lamps,** you were smart.

Vocabulary Exercise

Choose the correct word.

bother	1. We bought some _____ to make new curtains.
cloth	2. I'm going to _____ this Orlon sweater for a nylon one.
complaint	3. He works every evening at his _____ job.
exchange	4. Don't _____ me when I'm working!
loose	5. The farmer raises sheep and sells the _____.
part-time	6. She had a _____ about her room in the motel.
problems	7. They bought some _____ to build a bookcase.
toys	8. Please give the children these _____.
wood	9. Her sweater stretched, and now it's too _____.
wool	10. These math _____ are very complicated!

GRAMMAR

1. Simple conditions with *if*

Simple conditions tell about things that are true.
They have the simple present tense in each clause.
In these sentences, *if* means almost the same as *when*.

If you **wash** nylon pantyhose, they **don't shrink.**
This radio **plays** if it **has** batteries in it.

2. Possible conditions with *if*

Maybe something will happen. Then something else will happen.
Possible conditions tell about this.
Use a future tense, *can,* or *will be able to* in the main clause.
Use the simple present, simple past, present progressive, present perfect, or the future with *going to* in the *if* clause.

We**'ll return** the boots if they**'re** too tight.
Marion **can be** the manager if she **works** hard.
I**'ll be able to make** the dress if I **buy** a zipper.

If Kevin **cashed** a check, we**'ll have** money for dinner.
If you**'re** not **watching** that movie, **turn** the television off.
If the sweater **has stretched,** I **won't wear** it.
If Bill **is going to advertise** his car, he**'ll have to call** the newspaper.

Exercises

16A: **Conditions with *if*.** Choose a good ending for each sentence.

1. If you run out of gas,	a. we'll have to learn Spanish.
2. If we're going to Spain,	b. she'll soon get well.
3. If he cuts his finger,	c. the manager will return our money.
4. If you call the office,	d. you'll have to walk home.
5. If you don't heat the oven,	e. he'll need a bandage.
6. If he wears tight boots,	f. the receptionist will make an appointment.
7. If she takes her medicine,	g. his feet will hurt.
8. If the batteries are dead,	h. you won't be able to bake the cake.
9. If you complain too much,	i. the tape recorder won't work.
10. If we return the broken toy,	j. nobody will listen to you.

16B: **Possible conditions with *if.*** Ask and answer. Use Cue Book Chart 1.

2/go on a picnic
STUDENT A What are you going to do tomorrow?
STUDENT B If it doesn't rain, I'm going to go on a picnic.
STUDENT A What will you do if it rains?
STUDENT B I'll sleep all day.

1. **3**/repair the car
2. **4**/build a new porch
3. **6**/walk in the fields
4. **7**/cut the grass
5. **2**/ride a horse
6. **3**/work in the garden
7. **4**/drive to the country
8. **6**/go swimming
9. **7**/climb a mountain
10. **2**/pick raspberries

16C: **Possible conditions with *if.*** Make sentences. Use Cue Book Chart 2.

1/good food/always feel well
If you eat good food, you'll always feel well.

1. **2**/too much lemonade/get sick
2. **3**/cotton clothes/be cool in the summer
3. **4**/your car/be able to afford a vacation
4. **5**/an airplane/be able to fly to Acapulco
5. **6**/the most beautiful picture/win the prize
6. **7**/all these books/pass the test
7. **8**/Tom's motorcycle/be in trouble
8. **9**/the answers correctly/get a good grade
9. **10**/carefully/never have an accident
10. **1**/too much candy/have a stomach ache.

16D: **Possible conditions with *if.*** Ask and answer. Use Cue Book Chart 7.

a chair
STUDENT A Are you going to buy a chair?
STUDENT B Yes, if they have a nice wooden one.

1. a coat   2. some boots   3. a belt   4. a scarf   5. some pillows

16E: **Relative clauses with subject pronouns.** Ask and answer. Use Cue Book Chart 7.

TV/screen
STUDENT A Do you want a new TV?
STUDENT B Yes. I want one that has a large screen.

1. table/top
2. blouse/sleeves
3. clock/alarm
4. jacket/zipper
5. radio/batteries

16F: **Possible conditions with _if._** Change each sentence to a negative.

If he repairs the engine, he'll be able to drive to Washington.
If he doesn't repair the engine, he won't be able to drive to Washington.

1. If you get a full-time job, you'll have to work every day.
2. If she watches television too late, she'll be tired in the morning.
3. If they run out of cash, they'll have to use their credit cards.
4. If you wear your leather shoes in the rain, they'll get dirty.
5. If she wears her fur coat, she'll be warm.

16G: **Possible conditions with _if._** Answer the question. Use Cue Book Chart 8. Use an _if_ clause.

1. What will happen if the fat man sits down?
2. What will happen if the thief takes the jewelry?
3. What will happen if the girl in the shoe department tries to run?
4. What will the children in the toy department do if they have enough money?
5. What won't the customer in the suit department do if he's smart?

16H: **_Too_ + adjective + _to._** Ask and answer. Use Cue Book Chart 9.

move/bookcase/**2**
  STUDENT A Did you move the bookcase?
  STUDENT B No, it was too heavy to move.

1. stand on/ladder/**3**
2. break/string/**4**
3. use/knife/**5**
4. sit on/rock/**6**
5. lie on/stones/**7**
6. sleep on/couch/**8**
7. walk on/fence/**9**
8. swim across/river/**10**
9. wear/sweater/**11**
10. drill/tooth/**12**

COMMUNICATION PRACTICE

Guided Conversation

CUSTOMER I'd like to return this scarf.
  CLERK What seems to be the matter with it?
CUSTOMER Oh, there's nothing wrong with it. I just don't like Orlon scarfs.
  CLERK Do you want your money back?
CUSTOMER No. I'd like a wool scarf instead.
  CLERK Fine.

Activities

A. Ask somebody.

Have you ever returned anything to a store?
Why did you return it? Did you get your money back?

Maybe you can use . . .

expensive	torn
tight	broken
loose	ugly

B. Talk with somebody.

1. Your uncle gave you a sweater for your birthday. It's too tight, it's a terrible color, and it's wool. (You always sneeze when you wear wool.) Ask another student to take the part of a complaint department clerk. Tell him or her about the sweater and exchange it for a different one. (Look at Conversation 2 for ideas.)

2. Harry is very lazy. He doesn't like to work very hard. He's talking to Miss Swift, the manager of a toy store, about a part-time job. Miss Swift asks him, "How old are you? Where have you worked before? How many hours a week can you work?" Harry asks her, "How much will you pay me? Will I have a lot of vacations? Can I get free toys for my brothers and sisters? Can I sit down when I work?" You and another student perform this interview. (Don't be surprised if Harry doesn't get the job!)

C. What do you think?

Are clothes made of synthetic materials better than clothes made of natural materials? Why do you think so?

Maybe you can use . . .

sturdy	inexpensive
durable	comfortable
strong	washable
soft	beautiful

Self Test

Make a new sentence. Use *if.*

Maybe it will rain. I'll take my umbrella.
If it rains, I'll take my umbrella.

1. Maybe John has his credit card. He can pay for dinner.
2. Maybe I'll wear my wool sweater. I'll be warm.
3. Maybe she'll return the jacket. She'll get her money back.
4. Maybe the dishes are plastic. They won't break.
5. Maybe we don't have any homework. We can watch television.

LESSON 17

Thinking About Clothes

READING

Have you ever really thought about your clothes? Why do you wear certain things and not others? Why do people wear clothes at all? There are four main* reasons* for wearing clothes.

The first reason is to cover* our bodies. You can do this very easily. (Think of a bathing suit.) Then why do people usually cover most of their bodies? Because of fashion*. People of different times and places have different ideas about right and wrong clothes and about how much of the body to cover. In parts of India and North Africa, women cover their faces. For a long time, people in China thought it was wrong to show their feet, and until recently*, people in Europe and North America wouldn't show any parts of their legs.

The next reason for wearing clothes is protection*. Clothes protect* us from heat* and cold, snow and rain. Heavy clothes and sturdy boots protect people who work outside from mosquitos, sharp branches and stones, and wild* animals. Other workers* wear thick gloves and hard hats to protect them when they use machines*.

The third reason for wearing clothes is utility*; for example, to carry things. Years ago, everybody carried a bag or purse to hold food, money, and other useful things. Today, most clothing has pockets. A suit can have as many as ten—four in the jacket, four in the pants, and two in the vest*!

The last, and probably the most important, reason for wearing clothes is vanity*. People want to look good. They want to look the same as other people, but they also want to look different from everybody else. One man's dark suit can look like every other dark suit, but he can wear a bright tie or shirt to show his individuality*. Many teen-agers always wear blue jeans and T-shirts*, but each one's T-shirt is different from everybody else's.

Some people think your clothes tell others about you. Look at your clothes. Which of the reasons above tells, "Why are you wearing that?"

main important
reason(s) a thing that tells "why?"
to cover to put something over

fashion the things that are all right to wear

recently not long ago

protection See New Words.

to protect See New Words.
heat See New Words.

wild See New Words.

worker(s) a person who works
machine(s) See New Words.
utility being useful

vest(s) See New Words.

vanity being proud

individuality being different
T-shirt(s) See New Words.

Questions

1. What things do clothes protect people from?
2. What is one useful part of clothes?
3. How many pockets are there in your clothes today?
   What useful things do you have in them?

VOCABULARY

New Words

2. **T-shirt**

3. **vest**

1. She's **pretending** to be a mother.

heat, *n.* being hot: *We sat in the heat of the fire.*

ma chine′(s), *n.* a thing that has moving parts for doing work: *Cash registers, computers, and typewriters are useful machines.*

to pre tend′, *v. Let's pretend to be famous musicians.* See Picture 1.

to pro tect′, *v.* to keep safe: *Protect the baby's eyes from the sun.*

pro tec′tion, *n.* protecting; being kept safe: *He wore shoes to the beach for protection from the hot sand.*

to re fer′, *v.* to send for information or help: *Our teacher refers us to many good books.*

top′ic(s), *n.* the thing written or talked about: *Farming is the topic of his article.*

T′-shirt′(s), *n. She's wearing blue jeans and a yellow T-shirt.* See Picture 2.

vest(s), *n. He bought a red wool vest.* See Picture 3.

wild, *adj.* living or growing in the forests or fields: *Tigers are wild animals.*

Principal Parts of Verbs

base form	present participle	past tense	past participle
pre tend	pre tend ing	pre tend ed	pre tend ed
pro tect	pro tect ing	pro tect ed	pro tect ed
re fer	re fer ring	re ferred	re ferred

READING AND WRITING SKILLS

Paragraphs/Topic Sentence

You know that a paragraph usually discusses one idea. One sentence in a paragraph gives the most important idea in that paragraph. That sentence is the topic sentence. The other sentences all give more information about the topic.

When you tell about a person or thing for the first time in a paragraph, use a noun. After that, you can use pronouns to refer to the noun. When you start a new paragraph, use the noun again.

Exercises

17A: Paragraphs.

Look at the fifth paragraph in the article "Thinking About Clothes." What is the topic of that paragraph? Who does the word *they* in the third sentence refer to? Who do the words *he* and *his* in the fourth sentence refer to?

17B: Paragraphs. Read this paragraph and answer the questions.

Mrs. Jones described the thief to the police. He was short and fat, and he had red hair. He was wearing old blue jeans, a dirty red sweater, and leather boots. His left hand had a bandage on it, but he could use it easily.

1. What's the topic sentence of the paragraph?
2. Do all of the other sentences give information about the topic?
3. Who do the words *his* and *he* in the last sentence refer to? What does the word *it* in that sentence refer to?

17C: Paragraphs. Use each group of sentences to write a paragraph. Put the topic sentence first. Don't forget to indent.

1. a. He's 81 years old, but he looks very young.
   b. After the party, Mr. Johnson will think about it for a long time.
   c. His family is having a party for him tonight.
   d. Today is Mr. Johnson's birthday.
   e. Everyone will bring food and presents.

2. a. The brakes don't work right either.
   b. It ran all right for a week, but then everything began to go wrong.
   c. Last month my uncle bought a new car.
   d. Then it stops running after a few blocks.
   e. The engine makes a terrible noise when he starts it.

17D: Paragraphs.

Look at Cue Book Chart 8. Pretend to be one of the people in the picture.
Write a paragraph with the topic sentence *A funny thing happened at the department store yesterday* or *A terrible thing happened at the department store yesterday.*

COMMUNICATION PRACTICE

Writing Activities

A. Read the paragraph again about wearing clothes for protection. Write a paragraph about your clothes today. What do they protect you from?

B. Choose a person in your class and write a paragraph about him or her. Tell about the person's clothes, but don't tell his or her name. Read your paragraph to the class. Can anyone guess the person's name?

Unit Self Test

Choose a good ending for each sentence.

1. If you speak French in the English class,
2. If Bill has enough money,
3. If she wears a big hat,
4. If the sweater isn't washable,
5. If it doesn't rain,

a. you won't need your umbrella.
b. it will protect her from the sun.
c. nobody will understand you.
d. he'll pay the check.
e. I'm going to return it.

Make one sentence. Use *who* or *that.*

6. The horse is in the field. It runs fast.
7. The mechanic repaired my car. He's very pleasant.
8. The boy doesn't want to dance. He's wearing a blue T-shirt.
9. The girl is reading about bears. She likes wild animals.
10. The car wouldn't start. It belonged to the principal.

LESSON 18

That's impossible!

CONVERSATIONS

1.

OG What are you doing? Where's my breakfast?

ONA On the rock in the kitchen. There's a bowl of cold milk and a raw tiger steak.

OG You didn't answer my first question. What are you doing?

ONA What does it look like? I'm inventing the wheel.

OG The wheel? What do we need a wheel for?

ONA It'll be very practical. You'll see.

2.

OG What happened to the dead elephant that was in the field?

ONA I moved it.

OG You moved an elephant? Alone? That's impossible!

ONA Don't be silly. The other women helped me. Dead elephants are no problem since the wheel was invented.

3.

ONA What are you doing?

OG I want to be an inventor, too. I'm discovering fire.

ONA Fire?

OG Yes. We'll be warm all winter. And when food is cooked, it'll taste better than raw food.

ONA Cooked?

OG Just imagine. We can have toast, and baked bear meat, and hot tiger milk, and . . .

ONA I'll see you later.

OG Where are you going?

ONA To get the other women. If *you* discover fire, we'll need firefighters right away!

Questions

1. What did Ona invent? What did she use it for?
2. What does Og want to discover? What's he going to do with it?
3. Do you think a man or a woman invented the wheel? Why?

VOCABULARY

New Words

possible

impossible

a lone', *adv.* without help from others; without anyone else: *She did her homework alone.*

bar'ber(s), *n.* a person who cuts hair: *My cousin is a barber in a large shop.*

to clean, *v.* to make clean: *Please clean the floor.*

con ven'ient, *adj.* easy to use; easily done; useful: *It's convenient to live near the bus stop.*

dead, *adj.* not living: *The flowers in the garden are all dead.*

to de sign', *v.* to draw or plan for the first time: *The architect designed the new office building.*

to dis cov'er, *v.* to find out, see, or learn for the first time: *The scientist discovered a new star.*

e quip'ment, *n.* things to use; supplies: *He keeps his camera equipment in that leather bag.*

ex per'i ment(s), *n.* a test to find out something: *We did an experiment to measure the size of the room.*

fire'fight'er(s), *n.* a person who stops fires: *The firefighters put water on the burning building.*

to i mag'ine, *v.* to think; to have an idea: *She likes to imagine living on the moon.*

im pa'tient, *adj.* not patient: *He's always impatient when he has to wait.*

im pos'si ble, *adj.* not possible: *It's impossible for pigs to fly.* See the picture.

to in vent', *v.* to make or think of something new: *Who invented the telephone?*

in ven'tion(s), *n.* something invented: *The calculator was a useful invention.*

in ven'tor(s), *n.* a person who invents: *Who was the inventor of the automobile?*

to make' up', *v.* to invent: *The children made up a story about dancing bears.*

pa'tient, *adj.* calm; not angry about waiting; not excited about problems: *Our teacher is always patient with our class.*

pi'lot(s), *n.* a person who steers a plane or boat: *My uncle is the pilot of a passenger plane.*

pos'si ble, *adj.* able to be; able to happen: *It's possible to fly to Madrid.* See the picture.

prac'ti cal, *adj.* useful: *It's more practical to take a bus than to drive your car.*

raw, *adj.* not cooked: *It can be dangerous to eat raw pork.*

to save, *v.* 1. to make safe: *The firefighter saved the boy from the burning building.* 2. to keep: *I'm going to save some money for my vacation.*

sci′en tist(s), *n.* a person who knows about science; a person who works with science: *The scientist is studying the moon.*

ser′i ous, *adj.* important; not funny: *Bad brakes are a serious problem on a car.*

since, *conj.* after the time that; from the time when: *He's been home once since he moved to Europe.*

star(s), *n.* one of the small lights in the sky at night: *Can you count the stars?*

toast, *n.* pieces of bread that are brown from heating: *She likes butter on her toast.*

Word Study

no/not

That**'s no** problem. = That**'s not a** problem.
There**'s no** milk in the refrigerator. = There **isn't any** milk in the refrigerator.

im-/in-

The prefixes *im-* and *in-* mean "not."

impatient = not patient **in**expensive = not expensive
impolite = not polite **in**convenient = not convenient
impossible = not possible
impractical = not practical

Principal Parts of Verbs

base form	present participle	past tense	past participle
clean	clean ing	cleaned	cleaned
de sign	de sign ing	de signed	de signed
dis cov er	dis cov er ing	dis cov ered	dis cov ered
i mag ine	i mag in ing	i mag ined	i mag ined
in vent	in vent ing	in vent ed	in vent ed
make up	mak ing up	made up	made up
save	sav ing	saved	saved

Pronunciation Sentences with articles *a, an, the* before consonants and vowels

A tiger is ***an*** animal.
A hungry tiger is ***an*** angry animal.
An umbrella is ***a*** useful thing.
A university offers ***a*** one-hour course.
I found ***a*** hotel in ***an*** hour.
An engineer taught ***an*** important course.

The scissors were designed for ***the*** barbers.
The old house was saved from ***the*** accident.
The idea of ***the*** assignment was accepted.
The electric light was invented years ago.
The equipment was lost in ***the*** afternoon.
The useful words were spoken to ***the*** actors.

Vocabulary Exercise

Choose the correct word.

barber	1. The _____ man didn't want to stand in line.
convenient	2. It's _____ to live near your job.
designs	3. The scientists did some _____ on the moon rocks.
equipment	4. The _____ washed and cut my hair.
experiments	5. The _____ flew the plane over the city.
impatient	6. She looked very _____ when she talked about the accident.
pilot	7. He _____ all of his wife's letters.
possible	8. She _____ all of her clothes herself.
saved	9. Is it _____ to move that bookcase?
serious	10. Please put the cleaning _____ in the closet.

GRAMMAR

Active and passive voice

Usually in English sentences, the subject performs an action. (It does something.) The verb is in the **active voice.**

You **bake** bread in an oven.
Somebody **invented** the wheel a long time ago.

Sometimes, the subject of a sentence receives the action. (Somebody or something does something to it.) Then the verb is in the **passive voice.** The passive voice always includes a form of the verb *be* and the past participle.

Bread **is baked** in an oven.
The wheel **was invented** a long time ago.

All verb tenses can be used in the passive voice.

Present: Chinese **isn't taught** in our school.
Present progressive: Two scientists **are being interviewed** on TV today.
Past: A new star **was discovered** last week.
Past progressive: The costumes **were being designed** in the art class.
Future: An apartment building **is going to be built** on that corner.
Future: All the equipment **will be cleaned** by Monday.
Present perfect: Hamburgers **have** often **been served** in our cafeteria.

Exercises

18A: **Passive voice.** Ask and answer.

Greece/Greek
> STUDENT A What language is spoken in Greece?
> STUDENT B Greek is spoken in Greece.

1. Spain/Spanish
2. France/French
3. Holland/Dutch
4. Japan/Japanese
5. the United States/English

6. Germany/German
7. Brazil/Portuguese
8. Italy/Italian
9. Russia/Russian
10. Mexico/Spanish

18B: **Passive voice.** Ask and answer.

wheel/invented/a long time ago
> STUDENT A When was the wheel invented?
> STUDENT B The wheel was invented a long time ago.

1. story/made up/last night
2. invention/shown on TV/last week
3. pilot/interviewed/yesterday
4. book/written/last year
5. accident/discovered/at six o'clock

18C: **Passive voice.** Ask and answer.

packages/sent
> STUDENT A Have all of the packages been sent?
> STUDENT B Only one has been sent.
> The others will be sent later.

1. sandwiches/made
2. experiments/done
3. chairs/fixed
4. letters/written
5. sweaters/sold

6. shirts/washed
7. gifts/wrapped
8. pies/baked
9. costumes/designed
10. tests/corrected

18D: **Passive voice.** Complete the sentence. Use the correct form of the verb.

1. (invent)   Thousands of things have been _____ since 1900.
2. (clean)   All of the furniture has been _____.
3. (wash)   Some of the dishes haven't been _____.
4. (invite)   We've never been _____ to her parties.
5. (paint)   My bedroom has just been _____.
6. (heat)   The toast has been _____ in the oven.
7. (discover)   Have people been _____ on the moon?
8. (see)   This invention has never been _____ before.
9. (show)   That movie has been _____ on TV.
10. (put)   The equipment hasn't been _____ in the cabinet.

18E: **Passive voice.** Ask and answer. Use Cue Book Chart 1.

2/interviewed for the newspaper
STUDENT A Why are you so serious?
STUDENT B I'm going to be interviewed for the newspaper.

1. **3**/seen on TV
2. **4**/introduced to the president
3. **6**/asked about the accident
4. **7**/given a test
5. **2**/sent to the principal's office

18F: **Passive voice/relative clauses.** Make one sentence. Use *who*.

The firefighter broke her leg.
She was taken to the hospital.
The firefighter who broke her leg was taken to the hospital.

1. The barber always cuts my hair. He was fired yesterday.
2. The pilot was in the accident. He was interviewed on TV.
3. The boys won the game. They were given the prize.
4. The scientist discovered the star. She was introduced to the president.
5. The girl brought the present. She wasn't invited to the party.

18G: **Passive voice/relative clauses.** Make one sentence. Use *that*.

Some of the clothes are hanging in the closet.
They've been washed.
The clothes that are hanging in the closet have been washed.

1. Some books are on the desk. They've been borrowed from the library.
2. Some chairs were painted. They've been put on the porch.
3. Some islands were discovered. They haven't been named.
4. Some equipment was broken. It's been fixed.
5. Some ideas were practical. They've been written down.

18H: **Relative clauses with subject pronouns.** Choose a good ending for each sentence.

1. I like plants   a. that are free.
2. I like food   b. that have flowers.
3. I like dogs   c. that have funny stories in them.
4. I like books   d. that tastes good.
5. I like museums   e. that don't bite.

COMMUNICATION PRACTICE

Guided Conversation

REPORTER   I understand you're trying to invent a
            machine for students.
SCIENTIST   Yes, I am. It'll be finished soon.
REPORTER   What will it do?
SCIENTIST   It's going to do homework.
REPORTER   Do homework! What a great idea!
SCIENTIST   Yes. If it works, I'll be famous.
REPORTER   If it works, every student in the world
            will thank you!

Activities

A. Ask somebody.

Have you ever tried to invent anything? What was it? Did it work?

B. Talk with somebody.

1. Almost everybody can play some kind of game. Ask a classmate about his or her favorite game. Is it hard or easy to play? Is it possible to play it alone, do you play it with one other person, or is it played on teams? What equipment is needed to play it? Could he or she teach you the game?

2. There has been a terrible fire at a hotel. After the fire, a reporter interviews one of the firefighters. The reporter asks, "How did the fire start? How many firefighters came? How many people were in the building? How did you save them?" You and a classmate take the parts of the reporter and the firefighter and perform the interview. (The reporter will start the interview by asking, "What's your name? How old are you? How long have you been a firefighter?")

C. What do you think?

Some people think the wheel was the most important invention in history. Do you agree? What other invention do you think was as important as the wheel? Why?

Maybe you can use . . .

natural	convenient
artificial	practical
synthetic	useful
real	beautiful
instant	exciting

Self Test

Complete the sentence. Use the correct form of the verb.

1. (design)   Is the book going to be _____ on Friday?
2. (discover)   An island was _____ in the middle of the lake.
3. (invent)   When was the automobile _____?
4. (use)   Will the equipment be _____ by the firefighters?
5. (heat)   The toast is being _____ in the oven.
6. (make)   The sandwiches for the picnic haven't been _____.
7. (write)   The instructions were _____ on the tag.
8. (see)   Many kinds of animals can be _____ at the zoo.
9. (wear)   The costumes are being _____ in the play.
10. (ride)   That horse has never been _____.

LESSON 19

I had a terrible dream!

CONVERSATIONS

1.

EVELYN What's the matter? You look sleepy.

RAY I am. I was wide awake all night because of a dream.

EVELYN What was it?

RAY It was terrible. I was running through a strange city. And although I didn't live there, I was looking for my own house.

EVELYN That sounds confusing.

RAY It was. But that's not all. Then it got very cold and snowy, and I was being chased by a huge lion that was roaring and trying to bite me.

EVELYN How awful! Then what happened?

RAY I woke up and discovered my blanket was on the floor, and my cat was sitting by my bed and purring.

EVELYN So that explains the dream.

RAY Yes, but then I was so nervous that I couldn't go back to sleep.

2.

CARMEN I've started to dream in English. It's very discouraging.

GEORGE What's wrong with dreaming in English?

CARMEN Well, I always say such silly things.

GEORGE What do you mean? Do you insult people?

CARMEN No, but I get confused. Last night I dreamed that some tourists asked me about a store that had a sale on boats. I said, "Go to the lake. All the boats there have sails."

GEORGE That's kind of funny.

CARMEN It's not funny to be shouted at by a whole group of green people with six eyes!

GEORGE Green people?!?!

CARMEN Didn't I tell you? They were tourists from the moon!

Questions

1. Why did Ray dream about being cold?
2. What was Carmen confused about in her dream?
3. Has a dream ever made you so nervous that you couldn't sleep? What was it?

VOCABULARY

New Words

1. sail

2. The ball came **through** the window.

al though', *conj.* it's true but: *Although it rained, we went on a picnic.*

to ap pear', *v.* to be seen; to start to be seen: *The moon appeared from behind a cloud.*

be cause' of, *prep.* made to happen by: *They were unhappy because of the rain.*

both, *adj.* the two; the one and the other: *Both horses were white. n.* the two together: *Both of my sisters are tall.*

by, *prep.* 1. next to: *He's sitting by the window.* 2. See Grammar.

to chase, *v.* to run after to catch or hurt: *The dog chased the cat.*

to con fuse', *v.* to make (someone) not able to understand: *So many people talking at the same time confused me.*

to dis cour'age, *v.* to make sad; to make (someone) not hope: *Failing again and again discourages anybody.*

fa mil'iar, *adj.* known: *She has a familiar face. A knife is a familiar tool.*

far'ther, *adv.* more far: *She lives farther from school than I do.*

far'thest, *adv.* most far: *Who lives the farthest from the gym?*

fi'nal ly, *adv.* at last; at the end: *They finally found the lost children.*

in'ter est ed in, *adj.* liking to know about: *She's interested in science.*

kind' of, *adv.* a little: *I feel kind of sad.*

own, *adj.* belonging to: *This is my own book. We make our own bread.*

to purr, *v.* to make a sound in the throat: *Cats purr when they're happy.*

to re mind', *v.* to make (someone) think of something: *My mother reminded me to take my books. He reminds me of my uncle.*

to roar, *v.* to make a loud noise: *The lion roared. The wind roared at the window.*

sail(s), *n. That boat has two sails.* See Picture 1.

to set, *v.* to put in a place: *Please set your books down quietly.*

sleep'y, *adj.* ready to go to sleep: *She's sleepy because she got up so early.*

strange, *adj.* 1. not known: *There's a strange man at the door.* 2. not usually seen or heard: *There were strange noises in the forest.*

such, *adj.* very much: *It's such a hot day today!*

through, *prep.* from end to end; from side to side; from one side to the other: *We drove through a storm. He drilled a hole through the floor.* See Picture 2.

well-known′, *adj.* famous: *He's a well-known inventor.*

whole, *adj.* having all of its parts; full: *He ate the whole bowl of fruit.*

Idioms

He's **wide awake.**
She's **sound asleep.**

Word Study

back

go back to sleep = go to sleep again after waking up

Principal Parts of Verbs

base form	present participle	past tense	past participle
ap pear	ap pear ing	ap peared	ap peared
chase	chas ing	chased	chased
con fuse	con fus ing	con fused	con fused
dis cour age	dis cour ag ing	dis cour aged	dis cour aged
purr	purr ing	purred	purred
re mind	re mind ing	re mind ed	re mind ed
roar	roar ing	roared	roared
set	set ting	set	set

Pronunciation   Sentences with voiceless and voiced stops; intonation in series

The people are proud of these popular posters, paintings, and pictures.
Bill, Bob, and Barbara brought bananas, bread, and butter for breakfast.
Tom took a tent, a tire, and a tape recorder out of the tow truck.

Has Dave ever dreamed about dogs, dancers, dentists, or dictionaries?
In college, my classmates complained about clubs, clever conversations, and crowds.
Greg grows his groceries in the garden: green beans, grapes, garlic, and grapefruit.

Vocabulary Exercise

Choose the correct word.

appears	1. He worked all night, but he _____ finished his homework.
both	2. That song sounds very _____ to me.
familiar	3. She went to the museum because she's _____ art.
farther	4. That singer often _____ on television.
finally	5. Please _____ your wet boots on this rug.
interested in	6. My uncle is fat, but _____ of my aunts are thin.
reminded	7. The bank is _____ from school than the post office.
set	8. Our teacher _____ us of the test tomorrow.
through	9. Did she eat the _____ melon?
whole	10. They walked slowly _____ the park.

GRAMMAR

1. Passive voice

In sentences in the passive voice, a phrase with *by* names the person or thing that does something.

Our company will buy that old building.
That old building will be bought **by our company.**

Did the reporter interview the scientist?
Was the scientist interviewed **by the reporter?**

2. *So* + adjective + *that*

The elephant was very big. It couldn't get through the door.
The elephant was **so big that** it couldn't get through the door.

The beets tasted good. I ate all of them.
The beets tasted **so good that** I ate all of them.

Exercises

19A: **Passive voice.** Ask and answer.

machine/built/a man/a woman
    STUDENT A Was the machine built by a man?
    STUDENT B No, it was built by a woman.

1. prizes/won/a painter/an actor
2. book/written/a teacher/a student
3. children/saved/a firefighter/a policeman
4. animals/confused/the lights/the noise
5. island/discovered/a sailor/a pilot

19B: **Passive voice.** Make a new sentence.

Women often drive school buses.
School buses are often driven by women.

1. Dreams sometimes frighten children.
2. Reporters frequently interview inventors.
3. Architects usually design buildings.
4. Scientists often do experiments.
5. Cats rarely chase dogs.

19C: **Passive voice.** Ask and answer.

broke the lamp/the cat
    STUDENT A Who broke the lamp?
    STUDENT B It was broken by the cat.

1. built this car/a Japanese company
2. drew the pictures in this book/a well-known artist
3. wore this costume/a character in the play
4. ate the sandwiches/the barber
5. wrote the article/a famous scientist

19D: **Passive voice.** Make a new sentence.

Many dreams have been explained by <u>doctors</u>.
<u>Doctors have explained many dreams.</u>

1. The customers have been insulted by <u>that impolite clerk.</u>
2. The lazy receptionist has been fired by <u>the manager.</u>
3. Many students have been discouraged by <u>failing a test.</u>
4. That book has been read by <u>both the teacher and the student.</u>
5. The whole pie has been eaten by <u>the dog!</u>

19E: *So* + **adjective** + *that.* Ask and answer. Use Cue Book Chart 9.

knife/**5**/cut the fruit
    STUDENT A Is the <u>knife</u> <u>dull</u>?
    STUDENT B Yes, <u>it's</u> so <u>dull</u> that I can't <u>cut the fruit.</u>

1. scissors/**6**/give them to the children
2. ground/**7**/plant the garden
3. bed/**8**/sleep
4. road/**9**/drive down it
5. river/**10**/swim across it
6. boots/**11**/walk
7. coat/**12**/wear it
8. snow/**1**/feel it
9. car/**2**/push it
10. rope/**3**/use it

19F: *So* + **adjective** + *that.* Make one sentence.

Marty is confused. He set his cat on the table and gave his books some milk.
<u>Marty is so confused that he set his cat on the table and gave his books some milk.</u>

1. That machine is complicated. The inventor doesn't understand it.
2. Bill is poor. A thief gave him a watch and some money for the bus.
3. Carol is interested in music. She sleeps under her piano.
4. Tom is forgetful. He doesn't remember his own address.
5. This elevator is slow. Three people had birthdays before getting upstairs.

19G: **Prepositions.** Ask and answer. Use Cue Book Chart 10.

lion/walking/**1**/woods
    STUDENT A Did you see the <u>lion</u>?
    STUDENT B Yes, <u>it</u> was <u>walking</u> <u>through</u> the <u>woods.</u>

1. calf/standing/**2**/barn
2. bird/flying/**3**/house
3. clerk (f)/working/**4**/counter
4. barber (m)/driving/**5**/city
5. pig/stepping/**6**/mud
6. cat/sleeping/**7**/table
7. rabbit/jumping/**8**/river
8. boy/walking/**9**/street
9. dog/running/**10**/tree
10. actress/stepping/**11**/stage

19H: *a little/a few* Ask and answer. Use Cue Book Chart 5.

> STUDENT A Would you like <u>an appetizer</u>?
> STUDENT B Yes. I'd like <u>a few</u> <u>boiled shrimp</u>.
>
> STUDENT B Would you like <u>some soup</u>?
> STUDENT C Yes. I'd like <u>a little</u> <u>onion soup</u>.

1. entree
2. some vegetables
3. a cold plate
4. some dessert
5. a beverage

COMMUNICATION PRACTICE

Guided Conversation

CAROL What's the matter? You look sleepy.
MARK I had a terrible dream last night.
CAROL Oh? What happened?
MARK I dreamed I was being chased by a huge <u>cow</u>. I was running as fast as I could, but it was catching up to me.
CAROL How awful! Then what happened?
MARK I don't know. It <u>mooed</u> so loud that it woke me up!

Activities

A. Ask somebody.

What's the worst dream you ever had?

B. Talk with somebody.

1. Play "Twenty Questions" with your classmates. You pretend to be a well-known person (a popular singer, an actor, or somebody who appears on TV). Write the person's name on a piece of paper. Then your classmates have to ask you questions to find out the person's name. If they ask twenty questions and they can't guess, you win. (Some good questions are, "Are you a man? Do you sing? Do you appear on a popular TV show? Have you ever been in a movie? Are you famous for playing a sport?")

2. Jack likes Vera very much. He's asked her to go out with him several times, but she was always busy. Finally, she agrees to go to a dance with him on Friday, January 8, at 9:00. Jack is so excited that he gets confused and arrives at her house at 8:00 on Saturday, January 9. Vera is *very* angry because she waited for him all night on Friday. You and a classmate take the parts of Jack and Vera and perform their conversation. What does she say to him? What does he tell her? Will she ever agree to go out with him again?

C. What do you think?

What makes you feel discouraged?
What do you do to feel better?

Maybe you can use . . .

fail a test	talk to parents
be insulted	go out with
be sick	friends
be alone	listen to music
have a lot of	eat
homework	watch TV
lose a game	read a book

Self Test

Make a new sentence. Use *by* and the passive voice.

1. Policemen often chase thieves.
2. The sailors discovered the island.
3. Those architects have designed many office buildings.
4. Failing the test will discourage the students.
5. The teacher is going to correct the papers.

Make one sentence. Use *so . . . that.*

6. The man was confused. He got lost.
7. The girl was discouraged. She started to cry.
8. The boy was sleepy. He went to bed early.
9. The woman was bored. She went to sleep.
10. The food was strange. I couldn't eat it.

LESSON 20

What Do Your Dreams Mean?

READING

Scientists have proved* that everybody dreams. Many people don't remember their dreams, but everybody has at least* three every night.

Many things can influence* your dreams. For example, if your bedroom is very hot, you'll probably dream about being in the desert. If you're worried, you'll dream that something is chasing you. You want to run as fast as the wind, but your feet are too heavy to move. You want to shout for help, but you can't make a sound*.

When you feel good, you'll usually have very nice dreams. If you want something very much, your dreams can give it to you. For example, someone who is in love* will often dream about getting married*.

There are some dreams that almost everybody has. A lot of people dream they can fly. Many people dream about walking down the street without all their clothes on. Almost everybody dreams about falling.

One very common* dream is the "examination* dream." Many people have versions* of this dream. In one version, a student is taking an important test. However*, he's never been to the class, he's never seen the teacher, and he doesn't understand any of the questions. In another version, a student is going to take a test, but she can't find the correct room. Or maybe she gets to the room, but it's the wrong time and nobody is there. Dreams like this usually mean that you want to be successful*, but you're afraid you'll fail.

Some people think dreams can predict* the future. They say things like, "If you dream about a dog, you'll be lucky. If you dream about a cat, you'll be unlucky. If you dream about strawberries, you're going to take a vacation. If you dream about pineapples, you'll be successful in business*."

Do you remember your dreams? If you don't, try this. Keep a pencil and paper next to your bed. When you wake up, think about your dream and write it down right away. (You'll forget it if you wait.) Keep a "dream notebook." Maybe you can figure out the meanings of your dreams.

*to prove to show (a thing) is true

*at least no fewer than

*to influence to make (something) happen

*sound(s) See New Words.

*in love See Idioms.

*to get married See Word Study.

*common See New Words.
*examination(s) a test
*version(s) one way of describing something
*however See New Words.

*successful See New Words.

*to predict to tell about before

*business See New Words.

Questions

1. What are three dreams that many people have?
2. What can you do to remember your dreams?
3. Do you think dreams can predict the future? Why do you think so?

VOCABULARY

New Words

busi'ness, *n.* 1. work; job: *A carpenter's business is building.* 2. buying and selling: *That hardware store does a big business in tools.*

col'or ful, *adj.* 1. having a lot of colors: *She wore a colorful blouse.* 2. interesting or exciting: *She told colorful stories about her trip.*

com'mon, *adj.* often seen or heard: *Snow is common in cold countries.*

how ev'er, *conj.* but: *We arrived late for dinner; however, there was plenty of food for us.*

to mar'ry, *v.* to start to be husband and wife: *They plan to marry in the spring.*

shy, *adj.* not comfortable with people; easily frightened: *He's very shy, so he doesn't like parties.*

sound(s), *n.* a noise: *I didn't hear a sound.*

suc cess'ful, *adj.* having success: *The successful actor has played a lot of parts.*

Idiom

They're **in love.**

Word Study

***get* + adjective**

They're **getting married** next month. = They're going to marry next month.

Principal Parts of Verbs

base form	present participle	past tense	past participle
mar ry	mar ry ing	mar ried	mar ried

READING AND WRITING SKILLS

1. Figures of speech/personification

Good writers often use colorful language to make their stories and articles more interesting. Figures of speech are kinds of colorful language.

Some verbs and adjectives are usually used to describe people and animals. Using them to describe things that aren't living can make your ideas more interesting. This is called personification. Here are some sentences that use personification.

These rocks **have slept** in the hot desert for millions of years.
Yesterday, the sun **vacationed** behind the clouds.
The candle **stole** the night from the room.
The **thirsty** earth **waited patiently** for the rain.
The **unfriendly** fire **ate** the dry wood.

2. Figures of speech/similes

A simile shows that two things are alike by using *as*. Here are some common English similes.

as white as snow	as hard as a rock	as fat as a pig
as cold as ice	as big as a house	as pretty as a picture
as sweet as pie	as hungry as a bear	as red as a beet
as old as the hills		

Exercises

20A: **Figures of speech/personification.** Choose the most colorful verb.

advertised   **bit**   **borrowed**   **broiled**   **swam**

1. The thick, black smoke over the forest _____ a serious fire.
2. The vegetables _____ in a pool of butter.
3. The hot sun _____ the people on the beach.
4. A small cloud in the night sky _____ the moon for a minute.
5. The cold wind _____ the noses of the children who were playing in the snow.

20B: **Figures of speech/personification.** Choose the most colorful adjective.

angry　　　**friendly**　　　**lazy**　　　**sad**　　　**thirsty**

1. He waited a long time for the _____ elevator.
2. The birds made their home in the _____ tree.
3. The _____ desert waited for rain.
4. The people were afraid to swim in the _____ ocean.
5. The _____ gray clouds hung over the trees.

20C: **Figures of speech/similes.** Complete each sentence. Make it as colorful as possible.

1. Linda never works. She's as lazy as _____.
2. Tom is always polite. He's as pleasant as _____.
3. This table is very sturdy. It's as strong as _____.
4. Rose never talks to anybody. She's as shy as _____.
5. My car doesn't go very fast. It's as slow as _____.

COMMUNICATION PRACTICE

Writing Activities

1. Do you think dreams can predict the future? Write a paragraph that explains your ideas.

2. Write a paragraph that describes a room in your house. Use figures of speech to make your paragraph interesting.

Unit Self Test

Write each sentence in the passive voice.

1. Somebody invented the wheel a long time ago.
2. Somebody designed this machine for patient people.
3. Somebody stole the money from the cash register.
4. Somebody wrapped his leg in a bandage.
5. Somebody served boiled cabbage with the sausage.

Write each sentence in the passive voice. Use *by*.

6. The doctors discussed the dream.
7. The teacher corrected the tests.
8. The little boy tore the menu.
9. The mechanic repaired the car.
10. The angry woman returned the blouse.

APPENDIX

ABBREVIATIONS

adj.	= adjective	**fut.**	= future	**p.**	= past	**pron.**	= pronoun
adv.	= adverb	**m.**	= male (man)	**pl.**	= plural	**sing.**	= singular
conj.	= conjunction	**n.**	= noun	**prep.**	= preposition	**subj.**	= subject
f.	= female (woman)	**obj.**	= object	**pres.**	= present	**v.**	= verb

IRREGULAR VERBS

Base form	Simple past	Past participle	Base form	Simple past	Past participle
be	was/were	been	lie	lay	lain
begin	began	begun	lose	lost	lost
bite	bit	bitten	make	made	made
blow	blew	blown	mean	meant	meant
break	broke	broken	meet	met	met
bring	brought	brought	pay	paid	paid
build	built	built	put	put	put
buy	bought	bought	read	read	read
catch	caught	caught	ride	rode	ridden
choose	chose	chosen	ring	rang	rung
come	came	come	run	ran	run
cost	cost	cost	say	said	said
cut	cut	cut	see	saw	seen
do	did	done	send	sent	sent
draw	drew	drawn	set	set	set
drink	drank	drunk	shine	shone	shone
drive	drove	driven	show	showed	shown
eat	ate	eaten	shrink	shrank	shrunk
fall	fell	fallen	shut	shut	shut
feel	felt	felt	sing	sang	sung
find	found	found	sit	sat	sat
fit	fit	fit	sleep	slept	slept
fly	flew	flown	speak	spoke	spoken
forget	forgot	forgotten	stand	stood	stood
get	got	gotten	steal	stole	stolen
give	gave	given	swim	swam	swum
go	went	gone	swing	swung	swung
grow	grew	grown	take	took	taken
hang	hung	hung	teach	taught	taught
have	had	had	tell	told	told
hear	heard	heard	think	thought	thought
hide	hid	hidden	throw	threw	thrown
hit	hit	hit	understand	understood	understood
hold	held	held	wake	woke	waked
hurt	hurt	hurt	wear	wore	worn
keep	kept	kept	win	won	won
know	knew	known	write	wrote	written
leave	left	left			

GRAMMAR SUMMARY

1. Imperatives

Open the door.
Don't drop that radio!
Let's set the table.
Let's not go swimming.

Be quiet, children!
Don't be afraid.
Let's be friendly.
Let's not be late again.

Remember to call your parents.
Don't forget to buy a newspaper.
Be sure to bring your books.

Remember that school starts at nine o'clock.
Don't forget that I'm going to go with you.
Be sure that the TV is working.

2. Present tense of *be*

I am hungry.	**(I'm)**	**We are** early.	**(we're)**
You are tired.	**(you're)**	**You are** smart.	**(you're)**
He is late.	**(he's)**		
She is angry.	**(she's)**	**They are** brave.	**(they're)**
It is new.	**(it's)**		

I am not ready.	**(I'm not)**	**We are not** cold.	**(we're not/we aren't)**
You are not busy.	**(you're not/you aren't)**	**You are not** tall.	**(you're not/you aren't)**
He is not funny.	**(he's not/he isn't)**		
She is not thirsty.	**(she's not/she isn't)**	**They are not** helpful.	**(they're not/they aren't)**
It is not correct.	**(it's not/it isn't)**		

Are you ready?   Yes, **I am.** (No, **I'm not.**)
Is John late?   Yes, **he is.** (No, **he's not/he isn't.**)
Are the boys young?   Yes, **they are.** (No, **they're not/they aren't.**)

3. Past tense of *be*

I was a student
You were an actor.
He was a doctor.
She was a baby.
It was Friday.

We were friends.
You were beginners.

They were teachers.

I was not an artist.	**(I wasn't)**	**We were not** children.	**(we weren't)**
You were not an actress.	**(you weren't)**	**You were not** teen-agers.	**(you weren't)**
He was not a chef.	**(he wasn't)**		
She was not a nurse.	**(she wasn't)**	**They were not** salesmen.	**(they weren't)**
It was not a notebook.	**(it wasn't)**		

Were you a doctor?   Yes, **I was.** (No, **I wasn't.**)
Was John a painter?   Yes, **he was.** (No, **he wasn't.**)
Were the girls students?   Yes, **they were.** (No, **they weren't.**)

4. Simple present tense

I like tea.
You like coffee.
He likes lemonade.
She likes pop.
The cat likes milk.

We like dessert.
You like soup.

They like sandwiches.

I do not like to swim.	**(I don't)**	**We do not like** to work.	**(we don't)**
You do not like to study.	**(you don't)**	**You do not like** to ski.	**(you don't)**

He does not like to run.   (he doesn't)
She does not like to paint.   (she doesn't)   They do not like to hurry   (they don't)
The cat does not like to play.   (it doesn't)

Do you like lemonade?   Yes, I do. (No, I don't.)
Does Mary like to swim?   Yes, she does. (No, she doesn't.)
What do the boys like?   They like soup.

5. Present progressive tense.

I am reading.   (I'm)   We are running.   (we're)
You are skating.   (you're)   You are cheering.   (you're)
He is singing.   (he's)
She is dancing.   (she's)   They are working.   (they're)
It is barking.   (it's)

I am not reading.   (I'm not)   We are not running.   (we're not/we aren't)
You are not skating.   (you're not/you aren't)   You are not cheering.   (you're not/you aren't)
He is not singing.   (he's not/he isn't)
She is not dancing.   (she's not/she isn't)
It is not barking.   (it's not/it isn't)   They are not working.   (they're not/they aren't)

Are you reading?   Yes, I am. (No, I'm not.)
Is John singing?   Yes, he is. (No, he's not/he isn't.)
What's the dog doing?   It's barking.

6. Future tense with *going to*

I am going to study.   (I'm)   We are going to work.   (we're)
You are going to swim.   (you're)   You are going to practice.   (you're)
He is going to read.   (he's)
She is going to walk.   (she's)   They are going to eat.   (they're)
It is going to play.   (it's)

I am not going to study.   (I'm not)   We are not going to work.
                               (we're not/we aren't)

You are not going to swim.   (you're not/you aren't)   You are not going to watch.
                               (you're not/you aren't)

He is not going to read.   (he's not/he isn't)
She is not going to walk.   (she/ not/she isn't)   They are not going to eat.
It is not going to play.   (it's not/it isn't)   (they're not/they aren't)

Are you going to study?   Yes, I am. (No, I'm not.)
Is Mary going to walk?   Yes, she is. (No, she's not/she isn't.)
What's the cat going to do?   It's going to play.

7. Future tense with *will*

I will study.   (I'll)   We will work.   (we'll)
You will read.   (you'll)   You will dance.   (you'll)
He will eat.   (he'll)
She will leave.   (she'll)   They will sleep.   (they'll)
It will run.   (it'll)

I will not study.   (I won't)   We will not work.   (we won't)
You will not read.   (you won't)   You will not dance.   (you won't)

He will not eat.   (he won't)
She will not leave.   (she won't)   They will not sleep.   (they won't)
It will not run.   (it won't)

Will you study?   Yes, **I will.** (No, **I won't.**)
Will John eat?   Yes, **he will.** (No, **he won't.**)
What **will the horse do?**   **It'll run.**

8. **Simple past tense**
   I worked.   We cooked.
   You arrived.   You forgot.
   He called.
   She cheered.   They graduated.
   It rang.

   I did not work.   (I didn't)   We did not cook.   (we didn't)
   You did not arrive.   (you didn't)   You did not forget.   (you didn't)
   He did not call.   (he didn't)
   She did not cheer.   (she didn't)   They did not graduate. (they didn't)
   It did not ring.   (it didn't)

   Did you work?   Yes, **I did.** (No, **I didn't.**)
   Did Mary cheer?   Yes, **she did.** (No, **she didn't.**)
   What **did the bell do?**   **It rang.**

9. **Past progressive tense**
   I was reading.   We were studying.
   You were typing.   You were speaking.
   He was walking.
   She was working.   They were shouting.
   It was running.

   I was not reading.   (I wasn't)   We were not studying.   (we weren't)
   You were not typing.   (you weren't) You were not speaking. (you weren't)
   He was not walking.   (he wasn't)
   She was not working.   (she wasn't)   They were not shouting. (they weren't)
   It was not running.   (it wasn't)

   Were you working?   Yes, **I was.** (No, **I wasn't.**)
   Was Mary cheering?   Yes, **she was.** (No, **she wasn't.**)
   What **was the dog doing?**   **It was running.**

10. **Passive voice**
    Present: Chinese **isn't taught** in our school.
    Present progressive: The building **is being designed** by the architect.
    Past: A new star **was discovered** last week.
    Past progressive: The scientist **was being interviewed** by the reporter.
    Future: An apartment building **is going to be built** on that corner.
    Future: The equipment **will be cleaned** by the students.
    Present perfect: Hamburgers **have** often **been served** in our cafeteria.

11. **Transitive and intransitive verbs**
    Transitive: He**'s boiling** the water.
    Intransitive: The water **is boiling.**

12. **Infinitives**

of purpose: I'm going to the store **to buy** a cassette player.

Why do you need a cassette player? **To play** my new tape.

after adjectives: This car is easy **to drive.**

That mountain is too high **to climb.**

short form of: Did you do your homework? No, I forgot **to.**

13. *-ing* **verbals**

as adjectives: We listened to a **singing** waiter.

He slept in a **sleeping** bag.

The man **standing on the corner** is waiting for the bus.

as nouns: Playing chess is fun.

I like **swimming** and **sailing.**

They talked about **vacationing** in the mountains.

14. **Past participles as adjectives**

The **burned** meat tasted terrible.

Her **broken** leg hurts.

15. *make* **+ noun/object pronoun + adjective**

Running **makes Tom tired.**

The hot sun **made us thirsty.**

16. **Clauses**

after *think, be glad, be sorry:* I think **it's going to rain.**

We were sorry **you were sick.**

relative with subject pronouns: I talked to the dentist **who works in that clinic.**

He bought a computer **that plays music.**

The woman **who complained to the waiter** was very angry.

The dog **that bit the little boy** didn't hurt him.

conditional with *if:* Wool shrinks **if you wash it in hot water.**

We'll return the boots **if they're too tight.**

If the sweater has stretched, I won't wear it.

17. **Intensifiers**

We didn't go swimming because it was **very** cold out.

We didn't go swimming because it was **too** cold out.

We didn't go swimming because it was **so** cold out.

We didn't go swimming because it was **such** a cold day.

It was **too** cold **to** go swimming.

It was **so** cold **that** we didn't go swimming.

18. **Pronouns**

Subject pronouns	Object pronouns	Possessive adjective pronouns	Emphatic possessive pronouns	Reflexive pronouns
I	me	my	mine	myself
you	you	your	yours	yourself
he	him	his	his	himself

she	her	her	hers	herself
it	it	its	its	itself
we	us	our	ours	ourselves
you	you	your	yours	yourselves
they	them	their	theirs	themselves

19. Nouns

Singular	Plural	Singular possessive	Plural possessive
clerk	clerks	clerk's	clerks'
family	families	family's	families'
boss	bosses	boss's	bosses'
man	men	man's	men's
child	children	child's	children's
wife	wives	wife's	wives'
sheep	sheep	sheep's	sheep's

-er/-or nouns from verbs

help	helper	act	actor
dance	dancer	direct	director
hit	hitter	visit	visitor

20. Adjectives

	Base form	Comparative	Superlative
Irregular	bad	worse	worst
	far	farther	farthest
	good	better	best
	little	less	least
Group 1	bright	brighter	brightest
Group 2	big	bigger	biggest
Group 3	angry	angrier	angriest
Group 4	brave	braver	bravest
Group 5	afraid	more/less afraid	most/least afraid

Group 1

bright	hard	quiet	sore	
calm	high	rich	sour	
clean	light	rough	strong	
cold	long	round	sweet	
cool	loud	sharp	tall	
dark	low	short	thick	
dull	narrow	sick	tight	
fast	new	slow	warm	
few	old	small	weak	
fresh	poor	smooth	wild	
great	proud	soft	young	

Group 2

big	hot
fat	sad
flat	thin
glad	wet

Group 3

angry	dry	friendly	hungry	noisy	sleepy	thirsty
busy	early	funny	lazy	pretty	sorry	ugly
cloudy	easy	happy	lucky	shy	sturdy	windy
dirty	foggy	heavy	messy	silly	sunny	

Group 4

brave	loose
fine	nice
huge	safe
large	strange
late	wide
little	

Group 5

afraid	convenient	forgetful	patient	unafraid
alike	correct	frightened	pleasant	unfriendly
awful	dangerous	handsome	polite	unhappy
beautiful	delicious	helpful	popular	unimportant
bored	different	impatient	practical	uninteresting
boring	difficult	impolite	scared	unlucky
careful	durable	important	serious	unpopular
clever	excited	inexpensive	special	useful
colorful	exciting	intelligent	successful	well-known
comfortable	expensive	interested in	terrible	wonderful
common	familiar	interesting	terrific	worried
complicated	famous	nervous	tired	

21. Adverbs

with -ly:

calm	calmly
angry	angrily
safe	safely

	Base form	Comparative	Superlative
Irregular	badly	worse	worst
	early	earlier	earliest
	little	less	least
	well	better	best
Group 1	dark	darker	darkest
Group 2	angrily	more/less angrily	most/least angrily

Group 1

dark	light
fast	loud
high	low

Group 2

angrily	loudly	rarely
calmly	often	safely
carefully	pleasantly	seldom
easily	politely	sincerely
frequently	probably	slowly
happily	quietly	usually

ANSWERS TO THE SELF TESTS

Lesson 1
1. earth
2. registration
3. failed
4. grades
5. course
6. handwriting
7. tests
8. form
9. geography
10. science

Lesson 2
1. d
2. f
3. a
4. h
5. b
6. c
7. j
8. e
9. g
10. i

Lesson 3
1. I'm glad he didn't fail the test.
2. I'm sorry they don't plan carefully.
3. I think geography is interesting.
4. I'm glad I finished my homework.
5. I don't think the teacher's going to collect the papers.
6. c
7. a
8. e
9. b
10. d

Lesson 4
1. The books were boring to read. It was boring to read the books.
2. That motorcycle was dangerous to ride. It was dangerous to ride that motorcycle.
3. The engine was difficult to repair. It was difficult to repair the engine.
4. The English class was interesting to teach. It was interesting to teach the English class.
5. That water was safe to drink. It was safe to drink that water,

Lesson 5
1. always
2. rarely
3. usually
4. never
5. sometimes

Lesson 6
1. Speaking English is easy.
2. Going to the movies is expensive.
3. Riding motorcycles is exciting.
4. Having an accident is terrible.
5. Walking on the highway is dangerous.
6. Discussing school

is boring.
7. Giving good directions is hard.
8. Studying at home is helpful.
9. Getting lost is awful.
10. Driving at night is difficult.

Lesson 7
1. It's interesting to vacation in the mountains. Vacationing in the mountains is interesting.
2. It's terrible to fail a test. Failing a test is terrible.
3. It's boring to discuss automobiles. Discussing automobiles is boring.
4. It's easy to repair speedometers. Repairing speedometers is easy.
5. It's exciting to drive a powerboat. Driving a powerboat is exciting.
6. never
7. always
8. often
9. seldom
10. frequently

Lesson 8
1. b
2. d
3. g

4. a
5. c
6. h
7. e
8. j
9. f
10. i

Lesson 9
1. boiled potatoes
2. baked fish
3. broiled lamb chops
4. written recipe
5. stuffed squash
6. fried rice
7. mixed vegetables
8. broken eggs
9. cooked cabbage
10. sliced ham

Lesson 10
1. heated
2. falling
3. sliced
4. boiling
5. winning
6. swinging
7. lost
8. Typed
9. barking
10. cut

Lesson 11
1. myself
2. themselves
3. ourselves
4. herself
5. itself
6. herself
7. yourself
8. himself
9. yourselves
10. itself

Lesson 12
1. We were surprised

to find you here.
2. She was happy to help us.
3. They were surprised to win the game.
4. I was sad to hear about your broken leg.
5. He was sorry to be late.
6. The man using the drill is the dentist.
7. The woman filling the prescription is my aunt.
8. The boy waiting in the office has a toothache.
9. The girl talking to the receptionist wants an appointment.
10. The man reading the newspaper lives next door to us.

Lesson 13
1. myself
2. themselves
3. herself
4. himself
5. yourselves
6. The woman talking on the phone is the receptionist.
7. The man sitting in the office hurt his leg.
8. The girls standing in line want to buy tickets.
9. The boy sitting in the dentist's chair has a toothache.

10. The people eating in the restaurant are happy.

Lesson 14
1. a little
2. a few
3. a few
4. a little
5. a little
6. faster
7. worse
8. the loudest
9. better
10. the most/least carefully

Lesson 15
1. The teacher explained the exercise to the students who stayed after class.
2. She bought some pantyhose that were on sale.
3. Did you pick up the check that was on the hall table?
4. We talked to the travel agent who made the reservations.
5. He likes the short-sleeved shirt that's in the window.

Lesson 16
1. If John has his credit card, he can pay for dinner.
2. If I wear my wool sweater, I'll be warm.
3. If she returns the jacket, she'll get her money back.
4. If the dishes are plastic, they won't break.
5. If we don't have any homework, we can watch television.

Lesson 17
1. c
2. d
3. b
4. e
5. a
6. The horse that's in the field runs fast.
7. The mechanic who repaired my car is very pleasant.
8. The boy who doesn't want to dance is wearing a blue T-shirt.
9. The girl who's reading about bears likes wild animals.
10. The car that wouldn't start belonged to the principal.

Lesson 18
1. designed
2. discovered
3. invented
4. used
5. heated
6. made
7. written
8. seen
9. worn
10. ridden

Lesson 19
1. Thieves are often chased by policemen.
2. The island was discovered by the sailors.
3. Many office buildings have been designed by those architects.
4. The students will be discouraged by failing the test.
5. The papers are going to be corrected by the teacher.
6. The man was so confused that he got lost.
7. The girl was so discouraged that she started to cry.
8. The boy was so sleepy that he went to bed early.
9. The woman was so bored that she went to sleep.
10. The food was so strange that I couldn't eat it.

Lesson 20
1. The wheel was invented a long time ago.
2. This machine was designed for patient people.
3. The money was stolen from the cash register.
4. His leg was wrapped in a bandage.
5. Boiled cabbage was served with the sausage.
6. The dream was discussed by the doctors
7. The tests were corrected by the teacher.
8. The menu was torn by the little boy.
9. The car was repaired by the mechanic.
10. The blouse was returned by the angry woman.

VOCABULARY

The Arabic number after an entry represents the lesson in this book where the word or phrase is presented; a Roman number indicates the previous book where the word or phrase was introduced.

A

a, *adj.* I
able, *adj.* II
about, *prep.* I
above, *prep.* II
absent, *adj.* 2
accent(s), *n.* 3
— mark(s), *n.* 3
to accept, *v.* 2
accident(s), *n.* 6
accountant(s), *n.* I
to ache, *v.* 12
ache(s), *n.* 12
across, *prep.* II
to act, *v.* II
actor(s), *n.* II
actress(es), *n.* II
ad(s), *n.* I
to add, *v.* II
to address, *v.* II
address(es), *n.* I
adult(s), *n.* II
to advertise, *v.* 15
to afford, *v.* 5
afraid, *adj.* II
after, *prep.* I
afternoon(s), *n.* I
again, *adv.* I
age(s), *n.* II
ago, *adv.* II
to agree, *v.* II
air, *n.* 4
airport(s), *n.* I
aisle(s), *n.* 15
alarm clock(s), *n.* II
alike, *adj.* II
all, *pron.* I; *adj.* 12
— about II
— over II
— right I, 11
— the time II
almost, *adv.* II
alone, *adv.* 18

a lot of I
already, *adv.* II
alphabet, *n.* I
alphabetical, *adj.* 13
also, *adv.* 10
although, *conj.* 19
always, *adv.* II
and, *conj.* I
angrily, *adv.* II
angry, *adj.* I
animal(s), *n.* I
to announce, *v.* II
announcer(s), *n.* II
another, *adj.* II; *pron.* 5
to answer, *v.* I
— the phone II
answer(s) *n.* II
any, *adj.* I
anybody, *pron.* II
anymore, *adv.* 8
anyone, *pron.* 10
anything, *pron.* II
apartment(s), *n.* II
— building(s), *n.* II
to appear, *v.* 19
appetizer(s), *n.* 8
apple(s), *n.* I
application(s), *n.* II
to apply, *v.* II
appointment(s), *n.* II
April, *n.* I
architect(s), *n.* I
arm(s), *n.* II
around, *prep.* II
to arrive, *v.* II
art, *n.* II
article(s), *n.* II
artificial, *adj.* 8
artist(s), *n.* II
as . . . as, *adv.* II

to ask, *v.* I
asleep, *adj.* II
assignment(s), *n.* II
assistant(s), *n.* II
at, *prep.* I
— all, *adv.* 12
— first, *adv.* II
— last, *adv.* II
attendant(s), *n.* 4
audience(s), *n.* II
August, *n.* I
aunt(s), *n.* I
automobile(s), *n.* 4
avenue(s), *n.* II
awake, *adj.* II
award(s), *n.* II
away, *adv.* II
right—, *adv.* II
awful, *adj.* I
awfully, *adv.* 6

B

baby (babies), *n.* II
to back, *v.* II
— up, *v.* 6
back, *adv.* 6, 19
back(s), *n.* II, 4
backache(s), *n.* 12
backyard(s), *n.* II
bad, *adj.* II
badly, *adv.* II
bag(s), *n.* I
to bake, *v.* 9
ball(s), *n.* I
balloon(s), *n.* II
banana(s), *n.* I
bandage(s), *n.* 11
bank(s), *n.* I
barber(s), *n.* 18
to bark, *v.* I
baseball, *n.* I
basket(s), *n.* I
basketball, *n.* I
bathing suit(s),

n. I
bathroom(s), *n.* I
battery (batteries), *n.* 4
to be, *v.* I
— fired 14
— off/on II
— on TV II
to be born, *v.* II
beach(es), *n.* I
bean(s), *n.* I
bear(s), *n.* I
beautiful, *adj.* I
because, *conj.* I
because of, *prep.* 19
bed(s), *n.* I
bedroom(s), *n.* I
beef, *n.* 8
beet(s), *n.* 8
before, *prep.* I
to begin, *v.* II
beginner(s), *n.* II
beginning(s), *n.* II
behind, *prep.* I
to believe, *v.* 13
bell(s), *n.* II
to belong to, *v.* II
below, *prep.* II
belt(s), *n.* 15
bench(es), *n.* II
best, *adj.* II; *adv.* 14
better, *adj.* II, 12; *adv.* 14
between, *prep.* I
beverage(s), *n.* 8
big, *adj.* I
bike(s), *n.* I
bill(s), *n.* 15
bird(s), *n.* I
birthday(s), *n.* II
to bite, *v.* II
black, *n., adj.* I
blackboard(s), *n.* I
blanket(s), *n.* I

block(s), *n.* 6
blouse(s), *n.* I
to blow, *v.* I
blue, *n., adj.* I
blue jeans, *n.* II
boat(s), *n.* I
body (bodies), *n.* II
to boil, *v.* 7, 9
— over 9
bone(s), *n.* 11
book(s), *n.* I
bookcase(s), *n.* I
bookstore(s), *n.* I
boot(s), *n.* 15
bored, *adj.* 5
boring, *adj.* II
born
to be —, *v.* II
to borrow, *v.* 2
boss(es), *n.* II
both, *n., adj.* 19
to bother, *v.* 16
bottle(s), *n.* I
bottom, *adj.* II
bottom(s), *n.* II
bowl(s), *n.* I
box(es), *n.* I
boy, *interj.* 2
boy(s), *n.* I
bracelet(s), *n.* II
to brag, *v.* II
brake(s), *n.* 6
branch(es), *n.* II
brave, *adj.* II
bread, *n.* I
to break, *v.* II
breakfast(s), *n.* I
bridge(s), *n.* II
bright, *adj.* II
to bring, *v.* II
to broil, *v.* 9
broken, *adj.* II
brother(s), *n.* I
brown, *n., adj.* I
brush(es), *n.* II

to build, v. II
builder(s), n. II
building(s), n. I
bulletin board(s),
n. II
to burn, v. II
burned up, adj. 8
bus(es), n. I
— driver(s),
n. I
— station(s),
n. I
— stop(s), n. I
bush(es), n. I
business, n. 20
busy, adj. I
but, conj. I
butter, n. I
button(s), n. 15
to buy, v. I
buyer(s), n. II
by, prep. 11, 19
— car/bus II

C
cabbage, n. 8
cabinet(s), n. I
cafeteria(s), n. II
cage(s), n. II
cake(s), n. I
calculator(s), n. 2
calendar(s), n. I
calf (calves), n. 6
to call, v. I
to call up, v. II
caller(s), n. II
calm, adj. II
calmly, adv. II
camera(s), n. II
can/can't, v. II
can(s), n. II
candle(s), n. II
candy, n. 10
capital letter(s),
n. I
car(s), n. I
card(s), n. I
careful, adj. II
carefully, adv. II
carpenter(s), n. I
carrot(s), n. I

to carry, v. I
to cash, v. 15
cash, n. 15
— register(s),
n. 14
cashier(s), n. I
cassette(s), n. II
— player(s),
n. II
cast(s), n. II, 11
cat(s), n. I
to catch, v. I
— a cold 11
to catch up with, v. II
cavity (cavities),
n. 12
ceiling(s), n. I
center(s), n. II
cereal, n. 8
certain, adj. 13
certainly, adv. 2
chair(s), n. I
chalk, n. I
change, n. 15
to change clothes,
v. II
character(s), n. II
to charge, v. 15
to chase, v. 19
check(s), n. 8, 15
to cheer, v. II
cheese, n. I
chef(s), n. 9
cherry (cherries),
n. I
chess, n. I
chest(s), n. I, II
chicken(s), n. I
child (children),
n. I
chin(s), n. II
chocolate, n.,
adj. 9
to choose, v. I
chop(s), n. 8
chorus(es), n. II
church(es), n. II
city (cities), n. II
to clap, v. II
class(es), n. I
classmate(s), n. II

classroom(s), n. I
to clean, v. 18
clean, adj. I
clerk(s), n. II
clever, adj. II
to climb, v. II
clinic(s), n. 12
clock(s), n. I
to close, v. I
close to, prep. II
closed, adj. I
closet(s), n. I
cloth, n. 16
clothes, n. I
clothing, n. 15
cloud(s), n. I
cloudy, adj. I
club(s), n. II
coat(s), n. I
coffee, n. I
cold, adj. I
cold(s), n. 11
to collect, v. 1
college(s), n. II
color(s), n. I
colorful, adj. 20
to come, v. I
— in I
comfortable,
adj. 14
comma(s), n. 7
common, adj. 20
company
(companies),
n. II
to complain, v. 16
complaint(s),
n. 16
complicated,
adj. 14
computer(s), n. 2
to confuse, v. 19
contest(s), n. II
convenient,
adj. 18
conversation(s),
n. II
to cook, v. II
cook(s), n. I
cookie(s), n. II
to cool, v. 9

cool, adj. I
corn, n. I
corner(s), n. I
to correct, v. 1
correct, adj. II
to cost, v. II
costume(s), n. II
cotton, n., adj. 16
couch(es), n. I
to cough, v. 11
could/couldn't, v. II
counter(s), n. I
country, n. I
country (countries),
n. II
course(s), n. 1
cousin(s), n. I
cow(s), n. 6
cream, n. II
credit card(s),
n. 8
to cross, v. II
to cross your
fingers, v. 13
crowd(s), n. II
to cry, v. I
cup(s), n. I
curtain(s), n. II
customer(s), n. II
to cut, v. II
— out II
— up II

D
Dad, n. I
to dance, v. I
dancer(s), n. II
dangerous, adj. II
dark, adj., adv. II
date(s), n. II
daughter(s), n. I
day(s), n. I
dead, adj. 4, 18
dear, adj. I
December, n. I
to decide, v. 6
to define, v. 1
definition(s),
n. 13
delicious, adj. II
to deliver, v. II

dental, adj. 12
dentist(s), n. I
department(s),
n. II
— store(s), n. II
to describe, v. 1
desert(s), n. 5
to design, v. 18
desk(s), n. I
dessert(s), n. II
dictionary
(dictionaries),
n. II
did/didn't, v. I
dietician(s), n. I
different, adj. II
difficult, adj. II
dining room(s),
n. I
dinner(s), n. I
to direct, v. II
direction(s), n. II
director(s), n. II
directory
(directories),
n. I
dirt, n. 6
dirty, adj. I
to disappear, v. II
to discourage, v. 19
to discover, v. 18
to discuss, v. 1
dish(es), n. I
to do, v. I
doctor(s), n. I
dog(s), n. I
doghouse(s), n. I
door(s), n. I
down, adv., prep.
II, 6, 10
downstairs, adv. I
downtown, adv. I
dozen(s), n. II
Dr., n. I
drama(s), n. II
to draw, v. II
drawer(s), n. II
drawing(s), n. II
to dream, v. II
dream(s), n. II
dress(es), n. I

dresser(s), *n.* I
to drill, *v.* 12
drill(s), *n.* 12
to drink, *v.* I
drink(s), *n.* II
to drive, *v.* II
drive(s), *n.* II
driver(s), *n.* II
driveway(s), *n.* II
to drop, *v.* II
drugstore(s), *n.* I
to dry, *v.* II
dry, *adj.* II
dull, *adj.* I4
durable, *adj.* 14
during, *prep.* II

E
each, *adj., pron.* II
— other 2
ear(s), *n.* II
early, *adj., adv.* II
earring(s), *n.* II
earth, *n.* 1
easily, *adv.* II
east, *n., adv.* II
easy, *adj.* II
to eat, *v.* I
egg(s), *n.* I
eight, *adj.* I
eighteen, *adj.* I
eighth, *adj.* II
eighty, *adj.* I
either, *adv.* 6
elbow(s), *n.* II
electric, *adj.* 16
elephant(s), *n.* II
elevator(s), *n.* 15
eleven, *adj.* I
else, *adj.* 11
emergency
(emergencies),
n. 11
empty, *adj.* I
end(s), *n.* II
engine(s), *n.* 4
engineer(s), *n.* I
to enjoy, *v.* II
enough, *adj.* I
entree(s), *n.* 8
envelope(s), *n.* II

equipment, *n.* 18
eraser(s), *n.* I
escalator(s), *n.* II
evening(s), *n.* I
ever, *adv.* II
every, *adj.* I
— hour 12
everybody, *pron.* I
everyone, *pron.* 10
everything,
pron. II
except, *prep.* II
to exchange, *v.* 16
excited, *adj.* II
exciting, *adj.* II
to exclaim, *v.* II
exclamation
point(s), *n.* 7
Excuse me. I, 1
exercise(s), *n.* II
expensive, *adj.* I
experiment(s),
n. 18
to explain, *v.* II
eye(s), *n.* II

F
face(s), *n.* II
factory (factories),
n. II
to fail, *v.* 1
fair(s), *n.* I
to fall, *v.* II
fall(s), *n.* I
false, *adj.* II
familiar, *adj.* 19
family (families),
n. I
famous, *adj.* II
far away from,
prep. II
farm(s), *n.* 6
farmer(s), *n.* 6
farther, *adv.* 19
farthest, *adv.* 19
fast, *adj., adv.* 14
to fasten, *v.* II
fat, *adj.* I
father(s), *n.* I
favorite, *adj.* II
February, *n.* I

to feel, *v.* II
fence(s), *n.* II
few, *n., adj.* II
field(s), *n.* I, 6
fifteen, *adj.* I
fifth, *adj.* II
fifty, *adj.* I
to figure out, *v.* II
to fill, *v.* II, 12
to fill out, *v.* II
finally, *adv.* 19
to find, *v.* I
to find out, *v.* 2
fine, *adj.* I, 2;
adv. 2
finger(s), *n.* II
to finish, *v.* II
fire(s), *n.* II
firefighter(s),
n. 18
fireplace(s), *n.* I
fireworks, *n.* I
first, *adj.* II
at —, *adv.* II
first class, *adv.* 5
first-class, *adj.* 5
to fish, *v.* I
fish (fish), *n.* I
to fit, *v.* II
five, *adj.* I
to fix, *v.* I
flashlight(s),
n. II
flat, *adj.* 4
floor(s), *n.* I
flower(s), *n.* I
flu, *n.* 11
to fly, *v.* II
foggy, *adj.* I
food, *n.* I
foot (feet), *n.* II
for, *prep.* I
— example 10
— sale 14
for, *prep.*
of time II
forest(s), *n.* 5
to forget, *v.* II
forgetful, *adj.* 9
fork(s), *n.* I
form(s), *n.* 1

forty, *adj.* I
four, *adj.* I
fourteen, *adj.* I
fourth, *adj.* II
free, *adj.* 15
frequently, *adv.* 5
fresh, *adj.* 8
Friday, *n.* I
friend(s), *n.* I
friendly, *adv.* II
frightened, *adj.* II
from, *prep.* I
in front of,
prep. I
front(s), *n.* 4
— yard(s), *n.* II
fruit, *n.* I
— stand(s),
n. I
to fry, *v.* 9
full, *adj.* I
full-time, *adj.* 16
fun, *n.* I
— house(s),
n. I
funny, *adj.* II
fur, *n., adj.* 16
furniture, *n.* I

G
game(s), *n.* I
— show(s),
n. II
garage(s), *n.* I
garden(s), *n.* II
garlic, *n.* 9
gas, *n.* 4
— station(s),
n. 4
geography, *n.* 1
to get, *v.* II
— + *adj.* II
— better 12
— dressed 11
— married 20
— out of 14
— out of the
way 14
— undressed
11
— well 12

to get along with,
v. II
to get to, *v.* 3
gift(s), *n.* II
giraffe(s), *n.* I
girl(s), *n.* I
to give, *v.* II
— a party II
giver(s), *n.* II
glad, *adj.* 1
glass, *n.* I
glass(es), *n.* II
glasses, *n.* II
to go, *v.* I
— back to
sleep 19
— camping II
— on a picnic
II
— out with 2
— shopping,
skating, skiing,
swimming II
— to sleep II
God bless you. 13
going to, *v.* I
golf, *n.* I
good, *adj.* I
Good luck. II
to grade, *v.* II
grade(s), *n.* II
to graduate, *v.* II
graduation(s), *n.* 2
grammar school(s),
n. II
grandfather(s),
n. I
grandmother(s),
n. I
grandparent(s),
n. I
grape(s), *n.* I
grapefruit, *n.* 9
grass, *n.* I
gray, *n., adj.* I
great, *adj.* I
green, *n., adj.* I
grill(s), *n.* II
groceries, *n.* II
ground, *n.* II
group(s), *n.* II

to grow, *v.* II, 11
to guess, *v.* 4
guest(s), *n.* I
guitar(s), *n.* I
gym(s), *n.* I

H
ha! ha! *interj.* II
hair, *n.* II
half hour, *n.* II
hall(s), *n.* I
ham, *n.* I
hamburger(s), *n.* I
hammer(s), *n.* II
hand(s), *n.* II
to hand in, *v.* 1
handle(s), *n.* 15
handsome, *adj.* I
handwriting, *n.* 1
to hang, *v.* I
to happen, *v.* II
happily, *adv.* 14
happy, *adj.* I
hard, *adj.* II, 14
hardware store(s),
     n. II
hat(s), *n.* I
to hate, *v.* II
to have, *v.* I
     — fun I
     — a good time I
     — a party II
     — a picnic II
     — a sale on 14
     — time off II
to have to, *v.* II
he, *subj. pron.* I
head(s), *n.* II
headache(s), *n.* 12
headlight(s), *n.* 4
to hear, *v.* II
to heat, *v.* 9
heat, *n.* 17
heavy, *adj.* I
to help, *v.* I
help, *n.* II
helper(s), *n.* II
helpful, *adj.* II
her,
     poss. adj. pron. I
     obj. pron. I

here, *adv.* I
hers, *emph. poss.*
     pron. II
herself, *refl.*
     pron. 11
hey, *interj.* I
to hide, *v.* II
high, *adj., adv.* II
high school(s), *n.* II
highway(s), *n.* 6
hill(s), *n.* II
him, *obj. pron.* I
himself, *refl.*
     pron. 11
his,
     poss. adj. pron. I
     emph. poss.
     pron. II
history, *n.* II
to hit, *v.* I
hitter(s), *n.* II
to hold, *v.* II
     — on II
hole(s), *n.* II
home, *n.* I
homework, *n.* II
hood(s), *n.* 4
to hope, *v.* 12
horse(s), *n.* I
hospital(s), *n.* I
host(s), *n.* II
hot, *adj.* I
hot dog(s), *n.* I
hotel(s), *n.* I
hour(s), *n.* II
house(s), *n.* I
how, *adv.* II
     — + *adj.* II
     — long II
     — many I
     — much I
     — old II
however,
     conj. 20
huge, *adj.* II
hundred(s), *n.* I
hungry, *adj.* I
to hurry, *v.* II
in a hurry II
to hurt, *v.* II, 11

husband(s), *n.* I
hyphen(s), *n.* 3

I
I, *subj. pron.* I
     — beg your
     pardon. 14
     — see. II
ice, *n.* I
ice cream, *n.* I
idea(s), *n.* II
idiom(s), *n.* 10
if, *conj.* 16
to imagine, *v.* 18
impatient, *adj.* 18
impolite, *adj.* 14
important, *adj.* II
impossible,
     adj. 18
to improve, *v.* 2
in, *prep.* I
     — a hurry II
     — love 20
     — pain 11
     — trouble 10
to include, *v.* 10
to indent, *v.* 10
inexpensive,
     adj. 14
information, *n.* 15
inside, *prep.* II
instant, *adj.* 9
instead, *adv.* 9
instead of, *prep.* 9
instructions, *n.* 15
to insult, *v.* 14
intelligent, *adj.* II
interest(s), *n.* II
interested in,
     adj. 19
interesting, *adj.* II
to interview, *v.* II
interview(s), *n.* II
interviewer(s),
     n. II
into, *prep.* I
to introduce, *v.* I
to invent, *v.* 18
invention(s), *n.* 18
inventor(s), *n.* 18
invitation(s), *n.* I

to invite, *v.* I
island(s), *n.* II
it,
     subj. pron. I
     obj. pron. I
its, *poss. adj.*
     pron. I
itself, *refl. pron.* 11

J
jacket(s), *n.* I
January, *n.* I
jewelry, *n.* II
job(s), *n.* I
to joke, *v.* 5
juice, *n.* 9
July, *n.* I
to jump, *v.* II
June, *n.* I
junk, *n.* II
just, *adv.* 1, 5
     — right, *adj.* I

K
kangaroo(s), *n.* I
to keep, *v.* II
     — a secret II
     — your fingers
     crossed 13
kid(s), *n.* II
kilometer(s), *n.* 6
kind(s), *n.* II
kind of, *adj.* 19
kitchen(s), *n.* I
kitten(s), *n.* I
knee(s), *n.* II
knife (knives),
     n. I
to knock, *v.* II
to know, *v.* I

L
ladder(s), *n.* II
Ladies and
     gentlemen. II
lake(s), *n.* II
lamb, *n.* 8
lamb(s), *n.* 6
lamp(s), *n.* I
language(s), *n.* II
large, *adj.* II
to last, *v.* II

last, *adj.* I, II
     at —, *adv.* II
late, *adj., adv.* II
later, *adv.* I
to laugh, *v.* I
lawn(s), *n.* II
lawyer(s), *n.* I
lazy, *adj.* 10
leaf (leaves), *n.* II
least, *adv.* 14
leather, *n., adj.* 16
to learn, *v.* II
to leave, *v.* I
left, *adj.* I
leg(s), *n.* II
lemon(s), *n.* I
lemonade, *n.* I
less, *adv.* 14
lesson(s), *n.* II
let's I
     — see. II
letter(s), *n.* I, II
lettuce, *n.* I
librarian(s), *n.* II
library (libraries),
     n. I
license(s), *n.* 4
to lie down, *v.* 13
to lift, *v.* II
light, *adj.* I, II;
     adv. II
light(s), *n.* I
to like, *v.* I
like, *prep.* 6
line(s), *n.* 3
lines, *n.* II
lion(s), *n.* I
lip(s), *n.* II
to list, *v.* II
list(s), *n.* II
to listen, *v.* I
little, *adj.* I, 14
to live, *v.* II
living room(s),
     n. I
long, *adj.* I
to look, *v.* II
to look at, *v.* I
to look for, *v.* I
to look in, *v.* I
to look out, *v.* 6

loose, *adj.* 16
to lose, *v.* I
lost, *adj.* II
a lot of I
loud, *adj.* II;
  adv. 3
loudly, *adv.* II
lounge(s), *n.* I
to love, *v.* II
love, *n.* I
lover(s), *n.* II
low, *adj., adv.* II
lower, *adj.* 12
lucky, *adj.* II
lunch(es), *n.* I

M
ma'am, *n.* II
machine(s), *n.* 17
made of, *adj.* 16
magazine(s), *n.* I
to mail, *v.* II
mail, *n.* II
mailbox(es), *n.* I
mailman
  (mailmen), *n.* I
to make, *v.* I
to make up, *v.* 18
man (men), *n.* I
manager(s), *n.* 14
many, *adj.* I
map(s), *n.* II
March, *n.* I
market(s), *n.* I
to marry, *v.* 20
material(s), *n.* 16
math, *n.* II
May, *n.* I
May I help you? II
maybe, *adv.* I, 2
me, *obj. pron.* I
  —, too, II
meal(s), *n.* II
to mean, *v.* 1
to measure, *v.* II
meat, *n.* 9
mechanic(s), *n.* I
medicine, *n.* 11
to meet, *v.* I
meeting(s), *n.* II
melon(s), *n.* I

member(s), *n.* II
menu(s), *n.* I
messy, *adj.* I
middle, *adj.* II
midnight, *n.* II
mike(s), *n.* II
milk, *n.* I
million(s), *n.* II
mine, *emph. poss.*
  pron. II
minute(s), *n.* II
mirror(s), *n.* I
to miss, *v.* I
Miss, *n.* I
mistake(s), *n.* II
to mix, *v.* 9
Mom, *n.* I
Monday, *n.* I
money, *n.* I
monkey(s), *n.* II
month(s), *n.* I
moon(s), *n.* 5
more, *adv.* II
morning(s), *n.* I
mosquito(es), *n.* II
most, *n.* I;
  adv. II
motel(s), *n.* 5
mother(s), *n.* I
motorcycle(s), *n.* I
mountain(s), *n.* II
mouth(s), *n.* II
to move, *v.* I
mover(s), *n.* I
movie(s), *n.* I
Mr., *n.* I
Mrs., *n.* I
much, *adj.* I
mud, *n.* 6
museum(s), *n.* I
music, *n.* I
musician(s), *n.* I
my, *poss. adj.*
  pron. I
myself, *refl.*
  pron. 11

N
to name, *v.* II
name(s), *n.* I
napkin(s), *n.* I

narrow, *adj.* 6
natural, *adj.* 8
near, *prep.* II
neck(s), *n.* II
necklace(s),
  n. II
to need, *v.* I
neighbor(s), *n.* I
nervous, *adj.* II
never, *adv.* II
new, *adj.* I, 1
news, *n.* II
newspaper, *n.* I
next, *adj.* I
  — door 12
next to, *prep.* I
nice, *adj.* I
night(s), *n.* I
nine, *adj.* I
nineteen, *adj.* I
ninety, *adj.* I
ninth, *adj.* II
no, *adv.* I
no one, *pron.* 10
nobody, *pron.* II
noise(s), *n.* 4
noisy, *adj.* II
none, *n.* I
noon, *n.* II
north, *n., adv.* II
nose(s), *n.* II
not, *adv.* I, 18
note(s), *n.* II
notebook(s), *n.* II
nothing, *pron.* II
November, *n.* I
now, *adv.* I
  — and then II
number(s), *n.* I
nurse(s), *n.* I
nylon, *n., adj.* 16

O
ocean(s), *n.* I
o'clock, *adv.* I
October, *n.* I
of, *prep.* I
  — course 5
  — course not 9
office(s), *n.* I
often, *adv.* 5

oh, *interj.* I
oil, *n.* 4
OK, *interj.* I
old, *adj.* I, 2, 5
on, *prep.* I
  — sale 14
  — the way 2
  — time II
once, *adv.* II
one, *adj.* I
one(s), *pron.* I
one hundred,
  adj. I
onion(s), *n.* I
only, *adv.* I
onto, *prep.* II
to open, *v.* I
  — wide 12
open, *adj.* I
opening(s), *n.* II
operation(s), *n.* 11
operator(s), *n.* II
opposite(s), *n.* 2
optician(s), *n.* I
or, *conj.* I
orange, *n., adj.* I
orange(s), *n.,* I
to order, *v.* I
order(s), *n.* 13
Orlon, *n., adj.* 16
other, *adj.* II
other(s), *pron.*
  II, 5
our, *poss. adj.*
  pron. I
ours, *emph. poss.*
  pron. II
ourselves, *refl.*
  pron. 11
out, *adv.* 4
out of, *prep.* II
outside, *prep.* II
oven(s), *n.* 9
over, *prep.* I
to own, *v.* I
own, *adj.* 19
owner(s), *n.* II

P
to pack, *v.* I
package(s), *n.* II

page(s), *n.* I
pain(s), *n.* 11
to paint, *v.* II
paint, *n.* II
painter(s), *n.* I
painting(s), *n.* II
pan(s), *n.* I
pants, *n.* I
pantyhose, *n.* 15
paper, *n.* I
paper(s), *n.* II
paragraph(s), *n.* 3
parent(s), *n.* I
to park, *v.* II
park(s), *n.* II
parrot(s), *n.* I
part(s), *n.* II
part(s) of speech,
  n. 13
part-time, *adj.* 16
party (parties),
  n. I
to pass, *v.* 1
passenger(s), *n.* 5
patient, *adj.* 18
patient(s), *n.* 11
to pay for, *v.* II
pea(s), *n.* I
peach(es), *n.* I
pear(s), *n.* I
pedal(s), *n.* 4
pen(s), *n.* I
pencil(s), *n.* I
pepper, *n.* II
to perform, *v.* II
performance(s),
  n. II
perhaps, *adv.* 2
period(s), *n.* 7
person (people),
  n. I
pet store(s), *n.* I
to phone, *v.* II
phone(s), *n.* I
photograph(s),
  n. II
photographer(s),
  n. I
photography, *n.* II
piano(s), *n.* II
to pick up, *v.* I, 10

picnic(s), *n.* II
picture(s), *n.* I
pie(s), *n.* I
piece(s), *n.* I
pig(s), *n.* 6
piglet(s), *n.* 6
pill(s), *n.* 12
pillow(s), *n.* I
pilot(s), *n.* 18
pineapple(s), *n.* I
pink, *n., adj.* I
place(s), *n.* I
to plan, *v.* II
plan(s), *n.* II
plane(s), *n.* I
planner(s), *n.* II
plant(s), *n.* II
plastic, *n.,*
  adj. 16
plate(s), *n.* I
to play, *v.* I, 16
  — records/the
    guitar II
play(s), *n.* II
player(s), *n.* II
pleasant, *adj.* 14
pleasantly,
  adv. 14
please, I
plenty, *n.* 15
pocket(s), *n.* II
point(s), *n.* II
to point at, *v.* I
police, *n.* II
policeman
  (policemen),
  n. I
polite, *adj.* 14
politely, *adv.* 14
pool(s), *n.* I
poor, *adj.* I, II
pop, *n.* I
popular, *adj.* II
porch(es), *n.* I
pork, *n.* 8
possible, *adj.* 18
post card(s), *n.* I
post office(s), *n.* I
poster(s), *n.* II
pot(s), *n.* I
potato(es), *n.* I

potato chip(s),
  n. I
powerboat(s), *n.* I
practical, *adj.* 18
to practice, *v.* I
prescription(s),
  n. 12
present, *adj.* 2
present(s), *n.* II
president(s), *n.* II
to pretend, *v.* 17
pretty, *adj.* I
price(s), *n.* 15
principal(s), *n.* 2
prize(s), *n.* II
probably, *adv.* 12
problem(s), *n.* 16
program(s), *n.* II
to pronounce, *v.* 1
pronunciation(s),
  n. 13
to protect, *v.* 17
protection, *n.* 17
proud, *adj.* II
public, *adj.* II
to pull, *v.* II
puppy (puppies),
  n. I
purple, *n., adj.* I
to purr, *v.* 19
purse(s), *n.* I
to push, *v.* II
to put, *v.* I
  — on II

Q
question(s), *n.* II
question mark(s),
  n. 7
quiet, *adj.* II
quietly, *adv.* II
quiz show(s), *n.* II
quotation mark(s),
  n. 7

R
rabbit(s), *n.* I
radio(s), *n.* I
to rain, *v.* I
rain, *n.* I
to raise, *v.* II
rarely, *adv.* 5

raspberry
  (raspberries),
  n. 9
raw, *adj.* 18
to reach, *v.* II
to read, *v.* I
reader(s), *n.* II
reading(s), *n.* II
ready, *adj.* I
real, *adj.* 8
really, *adv.* II
to receive, *v.* II
receptionist(s),
  n. 11
recipe(s), *n.* 9
to recommend, *v.* 5
record(s), *n.* II
  — player(s),
    n. II
red, *n., adj.* I
to refer, *v.* 17
refreshments, *n.* II
refrigerator(s),
  n. I
to register, *v.* 1
registration, *n.* 1
rehearsal(s), *n.* II
to rehearse, *v.* II
to remember, *v.* II
to remind, *v.* 19
to rent, *v.* 6
to repair, *v.* II
to reply, *v.* II
reporter(s), *n.* I
rest, *n.* I
restaurant(s), *n.* I
to return, *v.* 12
ribbon(s), *n.* II
rice, *n.* I
rich, *adj.* II
to ride, *v.* I
ride(s), *n.* II
rider(s), *n.* II
right, *adj.* I, II
  — away,
    adv. II
  — here, *adv.* I
  — now, *adv.* I
to ring, *v.* II
ring(s), *n.* II
river(s), *n.* II

road(s), *n.* II
to roar, *v.* 19
to roast, *v.* 9
roast, *adj.* 9
rock(s), *n.* 5
to roll, *v.* II
roll(s), *n.* I
roller(s), *n.* II
roof(s), *n.* II
room(s), *n.* I
rope, *n.* II
rough, *adj.* II
round, *adj.* 4
rowboat(s), *n.* I
rug(s), *n.* I
rule(s), *n.* II
ruler(s), *n.* I
to run, *v.* I; 16
  — into 6
  — out of 4
runner(s), *n.* II

S
sad, *adj.* I
safe, *adj.* II
safely, *adv.* II
to sail, *v.* I
sail(s), *n.* 19
sailboat(s), *n.* I
sailor(s), *n.* II
salad, *n.* I
salary (salaries),
  n. II
sale(s), *n.* 14
salesman
  (salesmen), *n.* I
saleswoman
  (saleswomen),
  n. I
salt, *n.* II
same, *adj.* 2
sand, *n.* 5
sandwich(es), *n.* I
Saturday, *n.* I
saucer(s), *n.* I
sausage, *n.* 8
sausage(s), *n.* 8
to save, *v.* 18
to say, *v.* I
scared, *adj.* II
scarf(s), *n.* 15

scenery, *n.* II
schedule(s), *n.* 2
school(s), *n.* I
science(s), *n.* 1
scientists(s), *n.* 18
scissors, *n.* II
screen(s), *n.* 16·
screwdriver(s),
  n. II
seal(s), *n.* II
season(s), *n.* I
seat(s), *n.* 7
second, *adj.* II
secret(s), *n.* II
secretary
  (secretaries), *n.* I
to see, *v.* I; 12
  I — . II
  Let's — . II
seldom, *adv.* 5
to sell, *v.* I
seller(s), *n.* II
to send, *v.* I
September, *n.* I
serious, *adj.* 18
to serve, *v.* 8
to set, *v.* 19
  — the table II
seven, *adj.* I
seventeen, *adj.* I
seventh, *adj.* II
seventy, *adj.* I
several, *adj.* II
shade, *n.* II
shadow(s), *n.* II
shaker(s), *n.* 10
sharp, *adj.* 14
she, *subj. pron.* I
sheep (sheep),
  n. 6
sheet(s), *n.* I
shelf (shelves),
  n. I
to shine, *v.* I
shirt(s), *n.* I
shoe(s), *n.* I
shop(s), *n.* II
short, *adj.* I
shoulder(s), *n.* II
to shout, *v.* II
to show, *v.* II

show(s), *n.* II
shower(s), *n.* I
shrimp, *n.* I
to shrink, *v.* 16
to shut, *v.* II
shy, *adj.* 20
sick, *adj.* II
side(s), *n.* II
sidewalk(s), *n.* I
sign(s), *n.* I
signature(s), *n.* II
silence, *n.* I
silly, *adj.* II
since, *prep.*
    of time II;
    conj. 10, 18
sincerely, *adv.* II
to sing, *v.* I
singer(s), *n.* II
sink(s), *n.* I
sir, *n.* II
sister(s), *n.* I
to sit, *v.* I
    — down I
six, *adj.* I
sixteen, *adj.* I
sixth, *adj.* II
sixty, *adj.* I
size(s), *n.* II
to skate, *v.* I
to ski, *v.* I
skin, *n.* 12
skirt(s), *n.* I
sky (skies), *n.* I
to sleep, *v.* I
sleeping bag(s),
    n. I
sleepy, *adj.* 19
sleeve(s), *n.* 15
to slice, *v.* 9
sling(s), *n.* 11
slow, *adj.* 14
slowly, *adv.* 14
small, *adj.* II
small letter(s),
    n. I
smart, *adj.* II
to smell, *v.* II
to smile, *v.* I
smoke, *n.* 7
smooth, *adj.* II

to sneeze, *v.* 11
to snow, *v.* I
snow, *n.* I
so, *conj.* I;
    adv. 1
soap, *n.* II
    — opera(s),
    n. II
soccer, *n.* I
sock(s), *n.* I
soft, *adj.* 14
some, *n.* I
somebody,
    pron. II
someone,
    pron. 10
something,
    pron. II
sometimes, *adv.* 5
son(s), *n.* I
song(s), *n.* II
soon, *adv.* I
sore, *adj.* 11
sorry, *adj.* 1
to sound, *v.* II
sound(s), *n.* 20
sound asleep,
    adj. 19
soup, *n.* I
sour, *adj.* 9
south, *n., adv.* II
to speak, *v.* II
speaker(s), *n.* II
special, *adj.* II
special(s), *n.* II
speedometer(s),
    n. 4
to spell, *v.* II
to spill, *v.* 8
spoon(s), *n.* I
sport(s), *n.* II
spring(s), *n.* I
squash, *n.* 8
stadium(s), *n.* 2
stage(s), *n.* II
stairs, *n.* I
stamp(s), *n.* II
to stand, *v.* I
    — in line II
    — up I
star(s), *n.* 17

to start, *v.* II
statue(s), *n.* II
to stay, *v.* II
steak(s), *n.* I
to steal, *v.* 14
steam, *n.* 7
to steer, *v.* 4
steering wheel(s),
    n. 4
to step, *v.* 6
    — on the
    brakes 6
    — on the gas 6
    — on it 6
step(s), *n.* II
still, *adv.* II
stomach(s), *n.* 12
    — ache(s),
    n. 12
stone(s), *n.* II
to stop, *v.* II
store(s), *n.* I
storm(s), *n.* II
story (stories),
    n. II
stove(s), *n.* I
strange, *adj.* 19
strawberry
    (strawberries),
    n. 9
street(s), *n.* I
to stretch, *v.* 16
string, *n.* II
strong, *adj.* 14
stuck, *adj.* 6
student(s), *n.* I
to study, *v.* I
to stuff, *v.* 8
sturdy, *adj.* 14
suburb(s), *n.* II
success(es), *n.* II
successful, *adj.* 17
such, *adj.* 19
sugar, *n.* II
suit(s), *n.* I
suitcase(s), *n.* I
summer(s), *n.* I
sun, *n.* I
sunburn, *n.* II
Sunday, *n.* I
sunny, *adj.* I

sunshine, *n.* II
supermarket(s),
    n. II
supplies, *n.* 2
sure, *adv.* I, 2, 5;
    adj. II
to surprise, *v.* II
surprise(s), *n.* II
sweater(s), *n.* I
sweet, *adj.* 9
to swim, *v.* I
swimmer(s), *n.* II
to swing, *v.* 8
swing(s), *n.* I
syllable(s), *n.* 3
synthetic, *adj.* 16

T
table(s), *n.* I
tablecloth(s), *n.* I
tag(s), *n.* 15
taillight(s), *n.* 4
to take, *v.* I
    — a bath/
    shower 1
    — a course 1
    — the
    escalator/
    train/bus II
    — a look at II
    — medicine 11
    — off II
    — the part of 1
    — pictures II
    — a street II
    — a test 1
    — a vacation 1
to take care of, *v.* 14
to take it easy, *v.* 6
to talk, *v.* I
talk show(s), *n.* II
tall, *adj.* I
tape, *n.* II
tape(s), *n.* II
    — recorder(s),
    n. II
to taste, *v.* II
taste, *n.* II
taxi(s), *n.* I
tea, *n.* I
to teach, *v.* II

teacher(s), *n.* I
team(s), *n.* I
teen-ager(s), *n.* II
television, *n.* 16
to tell, *v.* II
ten, *adj.* I
tennis, *n.* I
tent(s), *n.* I
tenth, *adj.* II
terrible, *adj.* II
terrific, *adj.* 2
test(s), *n.* 1
than, *conj.* II
Thank you. I, 1
Thanks. I, 1
that, *pron., adj.* I
the, *adj.* I
theater(s), *n.* I
their, *poss. adj.*
    pron. I
theirs, *emph.*
    poss. pron. II
them, *obj. pron.* I
themselves, *refl.*
    pron. 11
then, *adv.* I
there, *adv.* I
there is/are I
these, *adj., pron.* I
they, *subj. pron.* I
thick, *adj.* 14
thief (thieves),
    n. 14
thin, *adj.* I, 14
thing(s), *n.* I
to think, *v.* II
third, *adj.* II
thirsty, *adj.* I
thirteen, *adj.* I
thirty, *adj.* I
this, *adj., pron.* I
those, *adj., pron.* I
thousand(s), *n.* II
thread, *n.* 16
three, *adj.* I
throat(s), *n.* 11
through, *prep.* 19
to throw, *v.* I
thumb(s), *n.* II
Thursday, *n.* I
ticket(s), *n.* I

to tie, v. II
  tie(s), n. I
  tiger(s), n. II
  tight, adj. 16
  time, n. I
  times, n. II
  tip(s), n. 8
  tire(s), n. 4
  tired, adj. I
  title(s), n. II
  to, prep. I
  toast, n. 18
  today, n. I
  toe(s), n. II
  together, adv. II
  toilet(s), n. I
  tomato(es), n. I
  tomorrow, n.,
    adv. I
  tongue(s), n. II
  tonight, adv. I
  too, adv. I, 6, 19
  tool(s), n. II
  tooth (teeth), n. II
  toothache(s),
    n. 12
  top, adj. II
  top(s), n. II
  topic(s), n. 17
  tourist(s), n. 5
  tow truck(s), n. II
  toward, prep. II
  towel(s), n. I
  town(s), n. II
  toy(s), n. 16
  traffic, n. II
  train(s), n. I
    — station(s),
    n. I
to travel, v. 5
  travel agent(s),
    n. 5
  tray(s), n. II
to treat, v. 14
  tree(s), n. I
to trip, v. II
  trip(s), n. II
  truck(s), n. I
    — driver(s),
    n. I

true, adj. II
  trunk(s), n. 4
to try, v. II
  T-shirt(s), n. 17
  tub(s), n. I
  Tuesday, n. I
to turn, v. II
    — around 6
    — in 6
    — right/left II
to turn off/on, v. II
  TV(s), n. I
  twelve, adj. I
  twenty, adj. I
  twice, adv. II
  two, adj. I
to type, v. II
  typewriter(s),
    n. II

U

ugly, adj. I
umbrella(s), n. I
unafraid, adj. II
uncle(s), n. I
under, prep. I
to understand,
  v. II
unfriendly,
  adj. II
unhappy, adj. II
unimportant,
  adj. II
uninteresting,
  adj. II
university
  (universities),
  n. II
unlucky, adj. II
to unpack, v. I
unpopular, adj. II
until, prep. II
up, adv., prep. II,
  6, 10
upper, adj. 12
upstairs, adv. I
us, obj. pron. I
to use, v. I
useful, adj. 15
usually, adv. 15

V

to vacation, v. 5
  vacation(s), n. I
  valley(s), n. 5
  vanilla, n., adj. 9
  variety show(s),
    n. II
  veal, n. 8
  vegetable(s), n. I
  very, adv. I
  vest(s), n. 17
  vinegar, n. 9
to visit, v. I
  visitor(s), n. II
  voice(s), n. II
  volleyball, n. I

W

waist(s), n. II
to wait for, v. I
to wait on, v. II
  waiter(s), n. I
  waitress(es), n. I
to wake up, v. II
to walk, v. I
  wall(s), n. I
to want, v. I
  warm, adj. I
to wash, v. I
  washable, adj.
    15
  wastebasket(s),
    n. I
to watch, v. I
    — out II
  watch(es), n. I
  water, n. I
  way(s), n. II,
    2, 10
  we, subj. pron. I
  weak, adj. 14
to wear, v. I
  weather, n. I
  Wednesday, n. I
  week(s), n. I
  weekend(s), n. II
  well, interj. I;
    adv. II; adj. 12
  well-known,
    adj. 19

west, n., adv. II
wet, adj. II
what, pron. I
  — about I
  — color I
  — for 2
  — kind of II
  — next 9
  — time I
wheel(s), n. II
when, adv. I;
  conj. II
where, adv. I
which, adj.,
  pron. II
while, n. 12
to whisper, v. II
to whistle, v. II
white, n., adj. I
who, pron. I
whole, adj. 19
whose, adj.,
  pron. II
why, interj. I, 4;
  adv. I
    — don't you?
    II
wide, adj. 6
wide awake,
  adj. 19
wife (wives), n. I
wild, adj. 17
will/won't, v. II
to win, v. I
wind, n. I
window(s), n. I
windshield(s),
  n. 4
    — wiper(s),
    n. 4
windy, adj. I
winner(s), n. II
winter(s), n. I
to wish, v. 5
with, prep. I, 8
without, prep. I
woman (women),
  n. I
wonderful, adj. I
wood, n. 16

wooden, adj. 16
woods, n. II
wool, n., adj. 16
to work, v. I, II, 16
to work on, v. II
worker(s), n. II
workman
  (workmen),
  n. I
world, n. II
worried, adj. II
to worry, v. II
worse, adj. II;
  adv. 14
worst, adj. II;
  adv. 14
would/wouldn't,
  v. II
to wrap, v. II
  wrapping(s), n. II
to write, v. I
    — down, v. 1
  writer(s), n. II
  wrong, adj. II

Y

yard(s), n. I
year(s), n. I
yellow, n., adj. I
yes, adv. I
yesterday, n.,
  adv. I
you,
  subj. pron. I
  obj. pron. I
young, adj. I
your, poss. adj.
  pron. I
yours, emph. poss.
  pron. II
yourself, refl. pron.
  11
yourselves, refl.
  pron. 11

Z

zebra(s), n. II
zero(s), n. I
zipper(s), n. 15
zoo(s), n. I

INDEX OF SKILLS